E E Nichols

Publishing
Jan. 6 - 67

TREASURY OF THOUGHT

DAGOBERT D. RUNES

Treasury of Thought

OBSERVATIONS OVER HALF A CENTURY

PHILOSOPHICAL LIBRARY
NEW YORK

Printed in the United States of America

*To the memory
of my son Eugene*

Where there are stronger
always stay with the weaker!

TREASURY OF THOUGHT

A

Abhorrence

The crime they abhor in generations gone, they overlook in their own, because its commission is veiled by a camouflage of contemporary civilization.

Ability

Is measured not by the greatness of the talent but by the purpose for which it is employed.

Abnormal

All great ideas and all great actors on the stage of history were abnormal. Was Beethoven normal? Or Michelangelo? Da Vinci, Socrates, or Mohammed?

They all went off the norm, driving themselves incessantly for what they thought was vital and essential. You may call them neurotics, if you wish. Surely their response to given impulses was undue, strikingly undue, in the eyes of living mediocrities.

:-:

The nights of the truly outstanding are inhabited by demons, idols and visions. But without their fantasies and dreams, what a dull place the normal era would be.

:-:

Treat gently the abnormal; he may carry some subtle talent under the cloud of his peculiarities.

Abolitionism
The white man took willingly the black man as burden, but hesitates to take him as friend.

Absence
Makes a good seasoning but a poor staple.

:-:

Absence increases fondness—and ends in forgetfulness.

The Absolute
As far as morals are concerned, what matters is only our awareness that they are relative to time, place and government.

Abstinence

If our authorities were really willing and capable of arresting all persons who ever have engaged in sexual practices with others than their married spouses, there would be very few left above the teen age who might justly escape indictment.

I certainly do not advocate promiscuity, but I state the above fact to establish that though "non-married" sexuality may often be in bad taste and muddled emotionally, sex per se is no crime as abstinence per se is no virtue.

Acceptance

By hasty multitudes is a point against rather than for an ism.

Accidents

Man proposes—and a blind goddess disposes.

Actions

Speak loud but sometimes a whisper is more welcome.

:-:

Wisdom without action is no better than daydreaming. I don't think much of the daydreamer who fancies himself a formidable hero, nor of sagacity that remains unmoved by the iniquities of the day.

Activism

To take a position in life you have to do more than just think. You have to be doing. Be it approval or disapproval you cannot clap only one hand.

Adherence

Preconceived notions are the hardest to give up.

Adjustment

The adjusted are so completely oriented within themselves that nothing can penetrate that wall of egocentricity except what they chew and digest.

Admiration

Is a balm when known, an offense when shown.

:-:

Who fails to admire will never love.

Adolescence

Neither infancy nor childhood, but adolescence is decisive in the making of man. The tastes, physical and mental, fostered in those days will determine the rest of the living years.

Adventure
Nothing is more intriguing than the soul of a fellow man.

:-:

Man will search for starlings in foreign lands and pay no heed to the lark at home.

:-:

The greatest adventures are experienced in the soul of man, not across oceans or deserts.

Adversity
Is God's helpmate and the Devil's hand-maiden.

Advice
Is poor service indeed if given by those who lack sense of direction.

:-:

Advice should be given by the example of the accomplished, not by one's own meagre experience.

Advisers
Fools are ever ready advisers.

Affectation

They act like characters in a book, only tl ₌y read the wrong book.

Affection

Affection is the only cure for a lonely soul.

Age

Is but one step from youth. Let the flippant remember they may even fumble that one.

:-:

Age is a time for work, since most of the pleasures of youth have guttered out.

:-:

Man's true age lies in the life span ahead of him, not the span behind him.

:-:

Age is no cause for veneration. An old crocodile is still a menace and an old crow sings not like a nightingale.

:-:

Age is wasted on the tired. It is the most precious time of life.

:-:

Wisdom grows with the years but not in a barren soul.

:-:

Gray hair is a sign of age, not wisdom.

:-:

Some days we are ten years older than on others.

:-:

A fool gets more hardened with age, a wise man gentler.

:-:

The greatest tragedy of old age is to live on into a generation without peers.

:-:

When we are young, we are many people; when we are old, we are only one.

:-:

The later years of life are not the declining but rather the *inclining* years—inclining to serenity, maturity, understanding and tolerance. Life in its fullness is reserved for maturity; still, youth craves more frolic and cheer. Hope and confidence make for the young even a drab

| 17

world panorama appear full of color and promise.

The makers of a better world were never the young, always the mature. See: Rousseau, Lincoln, Roosevelt, Tolstoy, Jefferson, Socrates, Moses, Pestalozzi, Spinoza, Gandhi, Lessing.

:-:

It is folly to expect of youth the making of a better tomorrow; there will be no better tomorrow unless we make it today.

Aggression
How quick the sand of life runs out, and even the wasting is made doleful by man's impatient eristics.

:-:

Is carried by the fever of hate, and this fever finds its way into the heart and the minds of the people, but it originates always in the blackness of dictatorial avarice.

Agnostic
A timid person attempting to hide his insecurity under a metaphysical cloak. He is gnostic about himself but agnostic about everything else.

:-:

Agnostics admit that the true nature of God eludes them, as it does all men; the cleric covers his doubts with a seminary certificate.

Agriculture
Is a profession, not a way of life.

Ahimsa
This, the Hindu principle of non-killing of cows and other animals, has led to the killing of hundreds of thousands of Indian Moslems who ignored it. How often a religious tenet so drifts away from the original spirit that it leads to its opposite.

Alchemy
Superstition of yesteryear is the science of today. What science of our time will be the superstition of tomorrow? Laugh not at yesterday; tomorrow may have the laugh on you.

Alcoholism
Society's legitimatized drug addiction.

:-:

A society that grows fat on liquor taxes has little moral justification to become violently legalistic about dry intoxication. For every delinquent pulling a knife because of heroin, there are ten thousand who do it because of whiskey. For every automobile accident caused by drugged lethargy, there are a thousand caused by whiskey. For every bodily debility created by morphinism, there are a hundred induced by alcoholism.

Alike

Like the leaves on a tree, we are all alike and yet all different.

Alms

Were the early expression of social consciousness. The man who refused giving them is the cynic of our era.

Amateur

It is by the quality of his mistakes that you recognize the amateur.

Ambition

Is a mongrel seed. You never know what will come of it until it is too late: the tree of life or poison ivy.

:-:

Great ambition has sometimes destroyed the

one it possessed, but raised mankind a step or
two.

:-:

The dust in the sarcophagus of the conqueror
differs not from the dust in the peasant's grave.
And all that sweat and pain and blood for a
few years of vainglorious adventure.

:-:

The mere denial of ambition is not virtue.
Virtue lies in the proper direction of ambition,
not in its suppression.

America

Was erected with material that the builders
had rejected: adventurers, refugees, criminals,
bonded persons, slaves, the hunted and the out-
casts. Its glory is the nimbus that forever hazes
about the down-trodden.

:-:

America has freed the world and the world
cannot forgive her for that.

Amusement

Is the keyhole through which you can watch
man unobserved.

Ancestor Worship

May not only lead youth to search amid their heritage for the lasting values, but may tend to make older people prove their virtues by today's deeds.

Ancestors

I wish it were possible to have one of our ancient ancestors, let's say from three thousand years ago, pay us a visit. Many of us would realize how little we have learned since in things that matter.

Ancestry

Is something we all have, but an odd few insist upon it as their very own.

Angels

May be a figment of imagination, but devils are for real; I have met too many of them to doubt it.

:-:

Angels are in the heavens, I am sure, because there are deeds done by mortals that are difficult to explain by the mortal nature of man. The angels of self-sacrifice and everlasting devotion, of courage and tenderness—they must be fluttering about in the winds high above, sometimes taking on the face of man and his flesh.

:-:

Why did the Lord make so few winged ones and so many that crawl?

:-:

I don't know if the angels have wings; I am sure the devils do, they move about so fast.

:-:

If God could make angels, why did He bother with men?

Anger
Who never feels anger never cares.

:-:

Anger is the big brother of compassion.

Animal
A tiger may be ferocious but only man carries grudges from kin to kid.

:-:

Man has succeeded in cowing almost every beast except his fellow man.

:-:

Animals have no conscience. If they did, they would be better than people.

:-:

Animals we all are, but they live for today, we for tomorrow.

Anthropomorphism
The Bible suffers from theological anthropomorphism and the Darwinian theorems from a scientific one.

Anticipation
Nothing really ever happens; anticipation is its own reward.

Antiquity
They talk down its glory to flatter their own drabness.

Apology
People will apologize for stepping on each other's toes, but not for crushing each other's hearts.

Apparel
The drab tunic of the proletarian dictators is no less offensive a mockery of good taste than the gaudy uniforms of the sheiks of Araby.

Apparitions

Frighten us no more. No ghosts can match the horrible deeds of those this side the grave.

Appetite

At the table of life some few forget in their hasty grab for wealth that shrouds have no pockets.

Applause

Plays the Siren on the ocean of life, sweet lips and subtle poison. Alexander, Attila, Hitler, Stalin—each sacrificed a generation on the altar of vanity.

:-:

Some can handle it and are stimulated— others just get drunk.

Approval

By a fool is worse than rejection by a sage.

Argument

Those who are dead-set to win are likely to mark their cards.

:-:

A knave can win over a sage, if a fool is the referee.

:-:

The philosophical mind never wishes to win an argument, but rather the truth.

:-:

Argument is a sure sign of conversation gone sour.

:-:

Some argue to prove a point, others to prove themselves.

Aristocracy

Leaning on ancestors proves most often that aristocracy hardly ever outlasts its first generations.

:-:

A horse does not become a thoroughbred by chewing its oats without snorting, nor a man by genteel handling of knife and fork.

:-:

What was good in aristocracies is long disappeared and what is left is good for nothing.

:-:

There are no old families. Some got at the moneybag sooner, that's all.

:-:

Those whose nobility is of their own making are the only true aristocrats.

:-:

Throughout European history the people were kept in such filth, disease and poverty that their oppressors sincerely felt themselves better because they did not smell nor work. The grand delusion of the parasitic blue blood.

:-:

The freedom of the people begins with the end of dynasticism, and it is time to remove the remaining, almost ludicrous vestiges of dynastic tradition, with their pretentious titles of Baron, Earl, Lord, Duke and Marquis, if for no other reason than for that of historic tidiness. That place for this theatrical humbug is not on the mantelpiece but on the trash heap. The farce of today's aristocracy is an ugly reminder of the days when the kings and their nobles grew rich and corpulent upon the sweat and the blood of the man of the street and the man behind the plow.

Arrogance
Will create, in the strong, distaste; in the

weaklings, admiration. What a weak era we live in.

:-:

A race-horse strut ill becomes a donkey.

Art

Is man's feeble effort to imitate the Lord. Looking at certain canvases, I wonder if the Master is flattered.

:-:

Dilettantes interpret art for art's sake as art for the artist's sake.

:-:

Art for art's sake is like cake for cake's sake. It has to please someone or it is just a ragout of ingredients.

:-:

Genius may be novel but novelties are not genius.

:-:

Art in its original meaning means ability, craftsmanship, such as the art of the physician, the art of the soldier, the art of the architect. Our century has given birth to an art that requires no ability, no talent, merely expression. Some aging juvenile drips paint on a canvas on the floor, or uses his brush as a dart, and that bit of suffering canvas hits a frame and a remarkable public.

:-:

Of late, even two beer cans on a wooden tray have been classified as sculpture if offered by the bearded ones. All these abstractionists have in common with painters and sculptors is a dirty smock.

:-:

The scope and purpose of art is pleasure; all these aesthetic dissertations are no better than that particular lady's talking away in the face of a beautiful sunrise.

Association
Does not prove guilt but it indicates affinity.

Astronomy
Is only the knowledge of the visible firmament. A new science is yet to come: the search for the worlds beyond our garland of galaxies.

Atheism
I hope for God's sake that He has not left

Himself with man alone but has in other spheres better sons.

:-:

God does not shun reason but evades the smart-aleck.

:-:

To be of no God and rely on clever opinions is like having many acquaintances and no friend.

Atheists
Are like the savage on an island who tells his family there is nothing beyond this rock but water and wind. One can live like that and die like that. But some of us have a hunch there is more to it than meets the eye and ear.

:-:

Atheists brag that they can get along without God; this is hardly a distinction in an era where very, very few pay the Lord more than a Sunday call.

:-:

Those who are not troubled by questions know all the answers.

:-:

Atheists are often enough shamefaced anti-theists. They wish no *Theos,* no God, no Principle to interfere with the petty advantages of their little existence.

:-:

They can't find God because they search for Him only in the narrow confines of their traditions.

:-:

The atheist steps on the hem of God and thinks he has stopped the heavens.

Attitude

To a goat the most delicate garden is just a grazing place.

Author

It is imagination that makes a writer, not schooling, and you can't teach the first.

:-:

Writing is a peculiar art. In dance, music design, architecture, sculpture, very few feel competent enough to step before the public. In writing almost everyone wants to get into the act. The pen is patient and the paper indifferent. So much goes into print, and by so many who are totally unable to write, yet who lack the resolve to put down the pen.

Authority

Must indeed rest on the majority, but on their reason, not their prejudice.

Authorship

Too many speak who should be listening; too many write who should be reading.

Autobiography

May be history, if offered forthright: Biography is mostly fiction, be it glib or ardent.

B

Baal

To understand the Baal of today you have to study the Baal of yesterday. How far away is Octavianus Augustus from Joseph Stalin? How far away is Ferdinand of Spain from Hitler? And still they are the same.

They beat their brothers to the ground and set their foot upon their necks and put them to servitude like cattle. There will come a time when all symbols of oppression will roll into the sand—crown and scepter and hammer and sickle as well.

Babes

The Bible says you get the truth from them. Perhaps—if you get to them before they learn the ways of man.

Baby

When you first see it newborn it already has a life behind it of three-quarters of a year. It has suffered thirst and hunger, heat and cold, sour, bitter and sweet, tiredness, discomfort, indigestion and perhaps toxic illness. Sometimes it even completes its life span without ever setting foot into our world of rock and ether.

Beast

Perhaps there are worlds where the insects are as large as our mammals and the mammals as small as our insects. Man's greatest enemy would still be his fellow man and not the wild beast.

Beauty

Needs no explanation.

:-:

Beauty travels on many levels. There is beauty seen by the heart, one seen by the mind, and one by the guts and sex glands. A steak can be beautiful and so can an architectural plan. I have even heard a physician exclaim: "What a beautiful eczema!"

Beggars

Are not the poor but the greedy.

Belief

Is measured by demonstration, not mere acceptance. Angels without wings are not in good faith.

Benevolence

Is the true ambrosia of the gods.

Bible

It is an odd book—the word of God, rituals of priests, legends, dull chronicles, and a sprinkling of childish lore—still, this poorly edited anthology has outlasted all the master epics. A book is just a bit of literature but the Bible is the very vessel of *Shechinah,* the spirit of man, between heaven and earth.

:-:

It is an unfinished book. Who dares to say that Israel has yielded its last prophet?

:-:

If the Book is not worth living by, it is not worth pretending by.

:-:

Let God speak through the Book and bid the priests be silent.

:-:

| 35

If the good Lord did not write the text, then King Solomon did, with some help from his father, David.

Big Men
Have the same problems as little ones, but on a greater scale.

Biographies
Are rarely worth reading. They are written by either flatterers or antagonists. At best they only give you the neighbors' opinion of the hero, or some imagined composite put together with clippings and transcripts. We often don't know what really motivates the soul of our nearest kin or acquaintance. Who dares to state with any degree of certainty what moved a man a century ago, a thousand miles away?

The biographer is like the man who longs to see the legendary lady in the castle window. She raises the blinds only when she is ready for you, all made up and dressed up and smiled up. From afar you can scarcely tell whether she is 17 or 70, and when you take a second look the blinds come down.

Birth Control
The churches have given up sundry of their

medieval aspirations, such as the curtailment of science and freedom of speech, but tenaciously they hold on to others, like the dissolution of marriages that have long ceased to have reality except on their ceremonial scrolls, or the salvation of the unwanted human race.

It is no longer necessary to kill an embryo in order to interfere with the destructive population explosion.

The beggarly sharecropper in Brazil, the poorly employed laborer in the metropolis of the Western world, the communal worker in the Far East, the idle in India—they keep on raising a crop of children that goes to seed in the weeds of their ill-attended lives.

Hundreds of thousands of embryos are clumsily aborted every year, bringing illness and death to desperate women of the disinherited classes. The wealthy can find a safer way; the poor are left to their primitive attempts.

The churches demand the continence of the poor while such is obviously unnatural, or the punishment of another family increase that is economically disastrous.

The sharecropper or day laborer who can barely feed four is compelled to half-starve eight or ten, and more.

The clerics, their heads in grossly misunderstood parchment, take it upon themselves to set the economy of a billion families in distress.

I do not know when God died and left bishops as His executors to interpret His Will and Testament.

I have yet to see His seal and signature on such documents as the bishops pretend to act upon.

I did, however, see His sign, undeniably so, in the laughing eyes of planned-for and well-cared-for infants.

I cannot imagine the good Lord delighting in a hundred million unwanted new-borns, their little bodies bloated from starvation, disease and lack of care.

I say, let the bishops go back to their parchments and let the world have only wanted children, wanted by their parents and thus wanted by the One whose countenance loves to shine upon a happy flock.

:-:

Some of God's self-appointed advocates take it upon themselves to wittingly discourage the scientific management of family increase. Quoting ill-interpreted passages from holy writ, the custodianship of which they pretend, they discourage by threat of damnation all sensible efforts on behalf of birth control.

I have rather doubted the authenticity of divine power over fertility which these graduates of theological seminaries allocate to themselves. But I am convinced that the good Lord would much prefer a small number of well-fed and well-clothed believers to uncontrolled masses of impoverished and starving multitudes.

Blasphemy

It is not the blasphemer God minds so much as the "protector" of His honor.

Blessing

I doubt if prayers can sway the Lord, but if love can move mountains it can touch the heavens.

Blind

Love may be blind, but hate sees what is not there.

Body Chemistry

Its influence upon mental structure is sharply emphasized in the sudden change of attitude in man and woman right after the culmination of the sexual act.

Book Reviewing

Is a profession in which those who flunk the course get to teach the class.

Books

Are like people: one man's revelation is to the other a meaningless bore.

:-:

Books are like people; it is not the number that matters, but the few that stand by.

:-:

Our libraries are getting bigger, which makes it more difficult to find a good book. The shelves are groaning under the pressure of clothbound nothingness.

:-:

A book is great by what you give to it, not take from it.

:-:

The truly great book does not find its readers, it creates them.

:-:

You may never find a friend, but you can always find a book. And with books as your

friends, you will not go through life a lonely
man.

:-:

Big books are like overgrown people—fine to
stare at but little else.

Books are the invisible tie between the people of the world. The Torah binds the Jews
as the Koran the Moslems and the Gospels the
Christian nations. Confucius bound the Chinese and so did Lao-tse and Buddha; until
such books were replaced by Marx's *Capital.*

The gods live in the books and where the
books disappeared, the gods went with them.
Gone are the Carthaginians, the Sumerians, and
all their minor deities that never had a book
of their own.

Books are all we have of the gods of the past,
and of the present as well. And so the Book
remains with us the ever-heritage of the tie
with the heavens. Take away the books and
you have a turmoil of people without unity
or direction.

:-:

Books are so long because the writers sell the
harvest before they separate the wheat from the
chaff.

:-:

Perhaps the books of meaning shall be bound in the scroll of antiquity to warn the reader they have been penned to touch the soul and not tickle the funnybone.

:-:

The influential book is not the one that reaches the surface of many, but the heart of a few.

:-:

Don't live by a book; the purpose of man is man.

:-:

What is disturbing in this contemporary phase of Western literature is not the existence of literary roaches; they have always been around, but they kept to their cracks. Now they come out into the open and want us to watch them on stage, in the recital hall and in the pages of what, amazingly, so many of our reviewers refer to as books.

Bore
No man is boring who speaks of what troubles him.

Boredom
In the land of the dullards, boredom is hardly noticed; it has never been really absent.

Borrowing

The lender may lose a friend but the indifferent will never have one.

Brainpower

Only a fraction of mankind's mental capacity is being used. The overwhelming bulk of the world's brainpower perishes unused because of totalitarian executions or war activities, because of a poverty-stunted literacy among seven-tenths of the population, and finally because of premature assignment to dulling labor. We are running the world on one cylinder instead of ten.

Bravery

Fear alone makes for bravery; the reckless show no virtue, only contempt.

Bribery

Let not the satiated judge the pressure of temptation suffered by the hungry.

Brotherhood

Who is not his brother's keeper belongs not to the family of man.

:-:

Be wary of the protagonist for the brotherhood of mankind; likely as not, he pleads for love in terms of abstract billions of unknown foreigners because he never learned to love a small handful of his own people.

Buddhism

In its essence rests on four great principles, those of kindness, pity, communal joy and equanimity. Unlike Christendom, it managed to gain and retain loyal adherents without benefit of rack and faggot.

C

Cabbalah

The secret book of Hebrew tradition had no single author, nor had Torah nor Talmud. Its many authors wrote with sagacity which was not theirs but rather the reflection of the Divine Intellect they venerated.

:-:

The Cabbalah teaches that in the realm of cognition and inner being there are ten different spheres. Not even all those who speak for truth see it on the same level.

Calmness

Let not the calm of indifference be mistaken for a mastered temper!

Candor

Some who wouldn't suffer a breeze delight in sending forth a tempest.

Candor is insolence in a Sunday suit.

Capitalism

Has the rich and the poor; Communism, the poor and the poorer.

:-:

I would rather take capitalism without a soul than Communism without a heart.

Care

Who does not care has no care.

Cathedral

The most imposing cathedrals are never too far from slums.

Causality

There are two causes of every effect; the visible one, and the real one.

Cause

It is a Cause that separates men from the mere mass.

46 |

Celibacy

Is not a virtue and eunuchs are not paragons of ethics.

Ceremony

Is the outward sign of an inward duty. Some who deride ceremonials are merely covering up the tracks of their own egotism.

Chabad

To understand the forces of the world is not enough. To gain access to the creative powers, the Cabbalah teaches, one must have wisdom and intuition (*chochma* and *bina*). Only the three combined—*chochma, bina, da-at (chabad)* —raise man above the material world.

Chance

Throws people together, man and woman, friend and foe. Chance makes kin and kings, a turned-up nose or a dusky skin, and places one's cradle in a mansion or a tent in the desert. From this unsorted mixture in the caldron of fate man draws his lot, his life and his luck. Yet some still like to think their dish was set out for them with deliberate intent by a providential hand.

Change

Friends, work, leisure, convictions—man moves in a circle. Happy the man who can when need be jump his track for a wider orbit.

:-:

You may change man's conduct but not his conscience.

:-:

No man is the same for more than a fortnight.

Character

Is hard to determine, there are so many layers of pretense and prejudice hiding the core. Scratch the surface and you'll find the good are not so good, the bad not so bad.

:-:

Character gets no better with age, only more pronounced.

:-:

Character shows its color by our sins, not our virtues. The latter are too bland and lily-like.

:-:

Suffering may not make character, but kindness will.

:-:

Character must be seen in everyday life, not just in its Sunday best.

:-:

Tell me what you read and I'll tell you what you are.

:-:

It is when a man is in power that he shows his true direction and the measure of his patience.

:-:

Mankind suffers from those sick in character, not sick in mind. Our mental healers tend the foibles of elderly ladies and frustrated men.

What ails our generation are the viciously detached, despotic and clever schemers who are driving the world from brink to brink.

Charity
Is not the effect of faith, it *is* faith.

:-:

Charity is the common denominator of all religions.

:-:

There is no charity so noble the cynic cannot impugn its motivation.

Chastity
Is honorable but charity is virtue come alive.

Cheerfulness
May be only a mood, but one for the better.

Childhood
The premature fruit may be much inferior to the slowly ripening.

Children
Emulate the prejudices and superstitions of their parents, rarely their wisdom.

:-:

The newborn starts off with a score of notches on which to hang the good things in life. Watch the community load him with prejudice, malice and superstition.

:-:

The wondrous adventures a child's mind can experience on a walk through a deserted, littered lot set between two old houses!

:-:

Our ancestors called their newborn boy *Kaddish,* the Holy One. The child was their link to living eternity. Those who spend their existence without a child have no share in the fate of tomorrow's world. They circle around themselves with their backs to the future generations.

:-:

To a child, its games of make-believe are as serious as our realities are to us. I sometimes wonder which of the two has more substance.

:-:

There are no children, only young people.

:-:

No one would undertake to raise horses without a solid study of husbandry; still people feel competent to raise children without bothering at all to properly prepare themselves.

Chivalry

The chivalry of the medieval ages was no more than arrogant horsemen riding roughshod over the poor of the land, the land of the innocent neighbor as well as that of the native sons. If these cavaliers went abroad with their artful weapons, hammered out of the poll taxes they took from the meager earnings of the serfs and laborers, they didn't go to serve the cause of goodness or justice or peace, but rather the irrepressible wish of their liege or their own for loot of land or loot of gold.

:-:

It may be that some of the epics and legendary tales involving the era of chivalry rate fair or even high as pieces of literature. But is the tune worthy of such a high price? Must truth and sheer humaneness be sacrificed as the price for these false, adulterated songs of romanticized glorification of kingly scoundrels and robber cavaliers?

Choice
At so many crossroads it's not a choice between good and bad, but between evil and greater evil.

Chosen People
The pagans and gentiles begrudge the Jews their claim to a heritage which they themselves have been rejecting for thousands of years.

:-:

The Jews chose God when no one else wanted Him.

:-:

The Lord is not selective; the people are.

Christhost

The greatest number of books have been written about one whom we know the least: Jesus Christ.

:-:

One cannot be a Christian while living the life of a pagan. If your heart is pagan and your deeds are pagan, you remain outside the Circle of Christ, which means Church of Christ, no matter what prayers your lips speak, nor what the ikon before which you kneel.

:-:

The Jews always have denied and forever will oppose the concept of God besides God. God is *Echod,* and One stands eternally for no more and no less, no picture of Him, no son of Him. This philosophy unendingly separates Judaism from Christianity.

:-:

If He came to earth today, He would never forgive us, in all His celestial beatitude, for the unspeakable atrocities perpetrated on His kin and the kin of His mother and His faithful believers. All the paternosters and all the hymns of all fifty thousand saints and all fifty thousand theologians and all the genuflecting of a billion

Christian knees, those alive today and those interred since the night of the catacombs, could not wash away the Jewish blood that is on Christian hands. If Jesus came to earth today, He would shrink from the Gothic cathedrals and the forest of church spires that carry the cross He took upon Himself that man might live a loving creature. Perhaps He would slink away to some little ghetto street in New York City, where there is a tiny ten-by-ten synagogue. And He would sit down with the other bearded Jews on the hard benches in this true house of worship. And He would read with the others from the ancient book of Moses, which, as He said, He came to fulfill and not to destroy—the book of Moses, written in the script He could understand, written in the spirit in which He lived and for which He died.

:-:

God lived with the world and its people for a million years before Jesus was born, so why begin time with the Son of God? Why not with God, the Father? There must have been good and evil before Christ came to earth; there must have been sin and repentance, devotion and derision, helpfulness and viciousness, manliness and gentleness and godliness; there must have been saints and thieves, lechers and ascetics, foul men and sound men, naïve men and critics, the Lord's servants and the Devil's henchmen.

:-:

There was a God before Jesus.

:-:

Millions have died for Him, but only a few lived for Him.

:-:

Jesus may have risen, but His followers stayed down.

:-:

It is the same family in Little Rock that genuflects to Christ in front of the altar and to Satan in front of the schoolhouse.

:-:

They suffer the cross He bore and go forth to impose His pains upon others.

:-:

If His followers had been won by the point of a sentence instead of a sword, Europe's history would have been less sanguinary.

:-:

If the Jews killed Jesus, how come He is still alive? And if He is living—and certainly He is —why blame the Jews? Unless to discredit them as a whole.

:-:

Those who believe in Christ cannot accept His assassination by Jews; those who assert He was killed a fugitive criminal do not believe Him Christ.

:-:

To those ardent in adoration and yet intolerant: Let them ask themselves how ardent they would have been had they met Jesus in His living days as a poor preaching wandering carpenter.

They knew Him only in the glory of millennia, not in the drabness of the life of poverty and rejection. Before they condemn His contemporaries, let them question their own faith and belief.

:-:

If Christ came back the second time, He would rise in Israel, where those of His kinfolk live whom the Christians failed to kill, and His tender voice would mouth the ancient Hebrew words of prayer and consolation.

If He were to come upon the high walls of

the Vatican and meet the Latin priests in their black and red cloth and hear the forbidding tongue of Rome, He, the son of God, would shudder at the memory of the Roman angry cross. What the Roman Bishops had done to the people of Israel in His name, He could never forgive.

The Christ Drama

The Vatican produced in the fourth century a grandiose drama, "the calumny against Jesus," in which the Jew is the archvillain, condemned in the end to eternal punishment. So monstrously malevolent is the Jew depicted therein that the wide audience of the play finds it natural that all the Jews' offspring are destined to eternal disgrace.

Such is the power of the play that it encouraged a hundred generations of believers to tread on the Jew like a serpent, garrot his children and burn his women and unarmed men as they never would a living hen or calf or goat.

Before the Christian world can redeem itself before God and man, it has to change this horrid play in which the Jew is the Devil incarnate.

The play is the thing, the script that opened the sluice of hate and acrimony in the great

Christian Colosseum and made the infuriated audience yell for the blood of the Jew.

Christianity

The first time a Christian child comes face to face with murder it is in the serene intimacy of religious teaching with the beloved, kindly, suffering face of the one murdered on a cruel cross. And the first time a Christian child comes face to face with a murderer, it's the Jew, whose face it can only identify with the Jew next door.

This shock of the first and immediate experience of murder writes itself indelibly in the naïve mind, rarely if ever to be obliterated by later-day theoretical weighing of doubtful facts and dark antiquity.

The child has become Christian and as such a detester of Jews.

The early horror of the Jew rarely leaves the Christian. It takes an accomplished mind to totally free itself of this early Christological impact.

It is only now, after two thousand years of spiritual and physical abuse, that the highest ecumenical authorities of the Catholic Church ponder, almost casually, if the whole tale of the Jew as Christ-killer be not only unhistorical but theologically incorrect.

There must be a stronger word to classify such "error."

:-:

The churches themselves have far too much emphasized the importance of the belief in Christ instead of the importance of the Christian deed.

Christians

Have failed for two thousand years to prove what Christ's teachings could do. From auto-da-fé to Auschwitz, a chain of *Miserabilia*. Nowhere else in history were such saintly words turned to such abuse.

:-:

A monkey can learn to bow before a cross, but it takes a life of kindness and generosity to be a true Christian.

Churches

Are like umbrellas: a torn one is still better than none.

:-:

Churches have lost the touch of the Divine and turned to book reviews and politics.

Cities

Are like people: some are noisy and soon forgotten, others live on for a hundred generations after their homes and temples and streets are covered by silent sands.

Citizens

The unprincipled make good citizens but bad people.

Civil Rights

Those who strain to hear a whisper from freedom infringed in our country seem to have deaf ears for the screams of freedom outraged abroad.

:-:

Civil rights do not include the privilege of undermining the inherent civility of democratic society.

:-:

Civil Rights are limited by civil duties.

:-:

When it comes to civil rights, some tend to make a molehill out of a mountain.

Civilization

Can be judged by the value it places on human life.

:-:

Civilization always seems to be at its peak to the present generation. I wonder what the ancients would say to our contemporary mass slaughters, torture and suppression.

Civitas Dei

The Lord will meet you halfway, but you must take the first step.

Classics

The devotion to classicism is given to most great men. It is their deep-felt urge to strengthen themselves on the ancient eras of heroism, virtue and faith.

:-:

There is so much trash being published today there is a danger it might become the classic of tomorrow.

Classroom

Why race one student against another in an alleged effort to improve their minds?

Sometimes the average classroom reminds me of the old Japanese clubbing tournaments:

you put ten people in a closed arena and let them beat their brains out until one of them comes out the winner. He is the class valedictorian.

It may even be true that the winner in this tournament is the man of the greatest prowess, and deserves a crimson laurel of Karate. But is this our intent, to raise an aristocracy of eggheads, and to the devil with the people?

Cleanliness
Is a sign of respect for fellow man.

:-:

Cleanliness is a consideration for others rather than onself. For that reason, uncivilized people commonly are unclean.

Clergy
The clergy spends too much time in the vestry and not enough in the street.

Clergyman
The preacher should be outstanding in Divine, not public, relations.

Clerics
It is astonishing with what assurance clerics

and preachers give forth with the wishes and precepts of God at Sunday services; as if they had just finished breakfast with the good Lord and undertaken to acquaint the parsonage with His desires.

Cleverness

Will set the mind ajar; wisdom will set it at rest.

:-:

Cleverness is a poor substitute for understanding.

:-:

Cleverness is competitive, wisdom never.

:-:

Cleverness comes with the body, wisdom from the Lord.

Closeness

The schemer who leads a man over a hidden manhole also walks arm in arm.

:-:

One is often closer to another century than his own.

:-:

Relatives *can* be close, but friends *are*.

Colonialism

In the Latin-American countries the European imperialists were expelled, but the ugly dualism of ruthless patricians on one, the palatial, side and hapless *favellas* demeaning millions of natives on the other, the slum side, still persists.

:-:

By and large, the colonizers of the fifteenth, sixteenth and seventeenth centuries, referring to themselves as missionaries and discoverers, were no more than gold-and-gem-greedy pirates flying the cross at the bow and the black skull at the masthead. The colonizers of the eighteenth century and the early nineteenth century were slave hunters and territorial expansionists, and those of later decades were in the race for new markets, new mines and new plantations.

The colonizers of the nineteenth century in its second half divided Africa and Asia as gentlemen would a common hunting ground.

But the hunt is over and the colored nations of Africa and Asia have learned to live on their feet instead of on their knees.

Color

Man was made of clay. Clay is black or red,

but never white. White man is a decadent creature, away from sun, wind and the sea.

Comfort

Is the small benefit we derive for the most part from the deadly application of progress in science.

Common Man

One is inclined to endow one's heroes with virtues they do not possess and one's scoundrels with faults they lack; as time goes on, the attributes diminish in sharpness and in the end the heroes are not so great and the scoundrels are not so puny.

Communism

Welfare without liberty is only a plush form of enslavement.

:-:

Communism is less a creed than an escape of the frustrated failure.

:-:

Communism has driven off the captains of industry and replaced them with captains of demagogy.

:-:

Communism began by incarcerating the few to free the many, and then enchained the many to protect the few.

:-:

One of the great moral calamities perpetrated by the Communists is their having driven millions of persons to a flight into conformism, that is, phlegmatic acceptance of any and all directives coming from above without any wish for examination or criticism.

:-:

Let's beware that in the struggle for the rights of man some do not usurp the rights over man.

:-:

Masterminds expropriated the state in the name of the people and then expropriated the people in the name of the state.

Companionship
No one can afford to go to hell in his own fashion; Hades admits sinners in pairs only.

Comparison
Is the mother of envy.

:-:

The great deeds are aroused by comparison. Free man endeavors to lead his life without comparison and thus without competition.

Compassion
Is the only one of the human emotions the Lord permitted Himself and it has carried the Divine flavor ever since.

:-:

Those who do not feel injustice done to others are not part of the play the Lord has been ever staging. They are mere walk-ons in the scenes of history.

:-:

It is a far cry from expressions of pity to acts of solidarity.

Competition
This would be a more tolerable world to live in if men would merely go about their tasks instead of trying to be better than their fellow men.

Compliment
A trick coin carrying on its reverse the face of slander; a flip of circumstances, and there it is.

Comrade

Watch out for the Utopian magician—he has an ax up his sleeve.

Comradeship

What some refer to as unity is often but a bond of common hatreds and prejudices.

Conceit

The hill of progress is a baffling climb: at every turn, it seems, we have reached the top.

:-:

Conceit is the little man's substitute for self-satisfaction.

Confession

Without repentance will institutionalize failings and pay sin a reward for pausing to consider.

:-:

Confession of an old sin neither improves nor elevates man; the task lies in facing honestly your present failings and egocentricities.

:-:

Innocence that can be bought by confession is no better than any other purchased virtue.

:-:

Confession may be good for the soul of the criminal but does little for the victim.

:-:

Confession is a clever device of church people to deliver into their hands the power to relieve an offender of his guilt.

:-:

It is a worthless hollow coin that they give you; neither God nor gold nor goodness are in back of it. It takes an awfully callous soul to practice such a pretense of taking repeated confessions from repetitive evildoers.

:-:

But the gullible never die out, and it is cheap enough to buy even the sham of forgiveness by a slick whisper of regret.

Confidence
Will reform more transgressors than punishment.

Conformism
In the land of the one-legged, the two-legged is a cripple.

:-:

Conforming with even an only suspected evil

is the opportunist's choice of the easy path instead of the right one.

:-:

Polemus pantum pater was correctly stated by Heraklitus. Strife is the father of all, certainly the father of progress. The greatest drawback in history has always been conformism.

:-:

Conformism is the philosophy of indifference.

:-:

Passion can elevate man if it is passion for a noble existence and an unencumbered society. Conformism is the coward's apology for his own indolence.

Conquest

To conquer one's lust may sober the libidinous; to conquer one's hate is virtue itself.

:-:

It appears that in history once an act of conquest has succeeded, the misdeed assumes the attributes of legitimacy. Traditional history appears to be the *de facto* recognition of every evil deed that failed to be stopped or eliminated.

Conscience

Human conscience is the only true moral guide, since all so-called ethical precepts, as well as religious commands, may be—and have been —turned as easily to evil as to good.

:-:

Conscience is not a soft pillow to sleep on but rather a bed of pangs and restlessness. Only the indolent can sleep when evil prowls in the night.

:-:

Law may be a guide, but conscience is a leader.

:-:

A good conscience that is readily silenced by superficial or false promises is no better than no conscience at all.

Consistency

Is the program of dull minds.

Consolation

At its deepest is silent.

Conspiracy

Ours is an age of conspiracy; no more is it the bulging prowess, the sharper blade, or the bluer strains of blood that claims a crown. It is the cunning tongue that sets a tyrant on the throne.

Constancy
It is easier to be constant in hate than in love.

Constitution
A constitution is never better than those subscribing to it.

:-:

Some of the worst tyrannies, such as those of Russia and China, have been built on the understructure of an almost perfect constitution.

:-:

A government is what it acts out, not what it pretends.

Contentment
Contentment is given only those who serve a cause.

:-:

Contentment forever eludes the seeker of self-satisfaction.

Controversy
Frequently divulges little about the issues at

stake, but much about the motives of those dis-
agreeing.

Conversation
Fixed ideas are the roadblock on the path of
discussion.

:-:

Conversation is only fruitful if all speak the
same language.

:-:

Those who make conversation destroy it.

:-:

Conversation is sterile when motivated thinking dominates.

Conversion
The great many conversions of Jews from
their ancestral faith are not indicative of their
lack of conviction, but rather of the relentless
severity of Christian pressure.

:-:

The Jew who becomes a Christian or a Mo-
hammedan or a Marxist because it admits him
to a plush job in Vienna or Moscow, is like the
rice-Christian in China—when the missionaries

ran out of rice the Chinese ran out of Christianity.

:-:

There is no need to drop Judaism for Christianity. Jesus never left the Jewish fold, but many times did the Christians desert Jesus. God lives in the faith of man, not in his churches.

:-:

If you don't find God in your own faith, you will not find Him in a borrowed one.

Converts

Torquemada and Hitler have made more converts of Jews to Christianity than all the missionaries of all times put together. Only dread and the rack could make them change the Star for a Cross and those who changed have not made Jewry poorer nor Christendom richer.

Convictions

Precious few are the masters of their convictions, great is the number of those mastered by them.

:-:

He who says his convictions can never be shaken rarely stands on solid ground.

Corn

Truth is often corny; so is the staff of life.

Cosmogony

They speak of the Origin of the Universe as if this tiny cosmos man sees were the Lord's sole domain.

God lives in infinite mansions man can neither see nor comprehend, and He is Being in essence, not to be fathomed or judged by animal creatures.

Man hunts and searches on his whirling globe and whenever he unearths a miniature truth within his environ, he thinks himself close to the peak of science. But this very pinnacle itself is only a speck of dust on the infinite plain of God's realm.

Cosmos

Physically, we are a swiftly deteriorating fungus settled on a dust particle whirling rhythmically in a black and empty barrel—I say "empty" because the distances between one tiny planet and the other are so gigantic that they are little different from stray, hardly visible dust-bits that an "empty barrel" contains.

And yet this fungus, riding for fleeting seconds on the dust of space, thinks his barrel a universe—nay, *the universe*.

Courage

If by some chance a true history of heroism were written, one would see a new array of faces that the world has kept in shadow: little men and women, from tents and huts and tiny flats, scrubwomen and peasants and clerks who suffered, sacrificed and gave their lives away for son of mother or friend. We have had a thousand histories of boisterous valiance, of herald, sword and crown—none yet of the humble carriers of the banner of courage.

:-:

Courage is the conquest of fear, or else nothing but devil-may-care.

:-:

Courage may sometimes be of doubtful issue, but cowardice never is.

:-:

It takes a few ribbons to make people die for their country. It takes much more to make them live for it.

Courtesy

May be a veneer, but neither is rudeness the real thing.

Courtiers

Of old curveted about in the pageant of a monarch; today they strut in military tunics around the party boss.

Cowards

May rise to heroism and heroes sink into oblivion, but dullards stay forever tepid.

Creation

Is sudden evolvement—evolution is slow creation. The riddle of creative nature is still with us.

:-:

Creation is so difficult to conceive and yet more so to deny.

:-:

Some want us to believe the whole solar system grew out of an idly floating gas bubble. Still, whence the bubble?

:-:

The earth could not have been more dismal and dank before creation, when God moved on the face of the waters, than it is now. However, today through its formless bleakness runs a crimson thread.

:-:

The worm in the stomach may have guessed from which glands the juices spring, perhaps also how they change and mingle and curdle. He may even reckon he knows the secret of creation.

:-:

No one knows how it all began, yet more theologians as well as geologists talk as if they had been present at the baptism.

:-:

If the Lord wanted to top his creation, why crown it with such as rapacious man?

Creator
Praising the Lord is demeaning the Creator.

Credulity
Among the educated there is no less of it than among the ignorant; the gullible of today, however, require of the accepted nonsense that it appear in a more intricate form.

Crime
Deserves punishment; however, our punishment is but another crime.

:-:

More crime is perpetrated within the law than without.

:-:

There are no great criminals, only greatly misfortuned individuals. All crimes fit all people under altered circumstances.

:-:

There is no crime so enormous that a better society could not have ameliorated it.

:-:

They hunt the thief of a stolen rooster and name cities after plunderers of a nation.

:-:

If crime did not pay, it would be much easier to combat.

:-:

Psychologists tend to ignore the fact that understanding the criminal's motivations does not eliminate crime.

Criminals
When grandfather was a boy in civilized Austria, a poacher was shot in cold blood for snaring a rabbit and in America a man was strung up for stealing a horse from the stable.

In these same countries men were perpetrating thousandfold deeds of evil—maltreating the weaker, robbing the poor and riding roughshod over the helpless—with little or no restraint or punishment by the law. The law seems to be little concerned over the oppression of the weak and indigent, but readily shows its teeth when the property code is in danger.

Somehow, to me the governor who shuts the schools so little black girls should not share in learning with the whites is a far greater criminal than the peasant who steals a bag of chicken feed.

:-:

Mao is living it up in the palace in Peking, the philosopher draws a fancy pension from a remarkably forgetful government; while the little peasant, the factory worker, the storekeeper all rot in jail.

It is the wrong people who occupy the jails of the world and the law is wrong that puts them there and keeps the real criminals out.

Critic
A eunuch judging a man's lovemaking.

:-:

A skydreaming eagle without wings.

He lacks the courage to write; the critic's box is safe.

:-:

A professional critic is like a professional mourner: his grievances are of dubious sincerity.

Criticism
Criticism is often furtive envy, veiled by dialectics.

Critics
Pygmies with poison darts live in the valley of the sleeping giants.

Crucifix
To the Jew is only a Roman gallows upon which the Christians have pilloried Jews in every generation of every century. There must be a better symbol for Christian love, charity and forgiveness than the gallows.

Crucifixion
Man is most readily given to hate; it is high time that the crucifixion of the noble Jew Jesus be not a focal point of Jew hatred, but a beacon of that loving humility so close to the heart of the Nazarene.

Cruelty

Is not the beast in man, it is man in man. Animals know not cruelty, merely indifference.

:-:

Cruelty is the coward's defense.

:-:

Although they know hunger and fear, dumb animals know no cruelty; it takes training to make man evil, snide and cruel.

Crusaders

If the desire of the Crusaders was to preserve Christian relics, documents and holy places, it must be said that during their occupation of Jerusalem they displayed hardly any interest in the project, nor did the nobility that led these expeditions have even the reading capacity to understand such matters.

:-:

When the Crusaders captured Jerusalem they removed their shoes and sang Hosannahs: "Jerusalem, lift up thine eyes and behold thy liberators." And then they went on slaughtering the pagans. They herded all the Jews they could capture into the great synagogue in Jerusalem, and burned them alive.

Thereupon they staged a great procession to

the Holy Sepulcher singing, with tears in their eyes and a sob of joy in their throats—"Te Deum."

:-:

The two hundred years of crusading brought to the peoples of Eastern Europe and Western Asia war and devastation at the hands of greedy expansionists, who carried a cross on their shoulders and a devil in their hearts. Along this *via dolorosa,* whose stages are marked by the enslavement of children, the burning of Constantinople and the ravaging of the Balkans, lie tens of thousands of Jewish gravestones—mute evidence of man's inhumanity to man.

Crusades

When the Mongols threatened the power of Islam, many of Europe's princes saw an opportunity to benefit from this turmoil in the Orient, and initiated a score of Crusades for the protection of alleged relics.

There is no Grail in the Vatican and no cloak of Jesus; yet there was enough timber from the Cross in the abbeys, churches and chapels of medieval Europe to erect a forest of gallows. But on their way to Jerusalem the unholy Crusaders filled the rivers of France and

Germany with floating Jewish corpses and crucified the kin of Christ a thousand times over.

Culture
The culture of a nation is judged not by what its scholars think but by what its little people think, just as its organization is judged not by how its rich live but by how its poor live.

:-:

The culture of a nation is to be judged by the standards of its wide masses, not those of the upper strata.

Curiosity
Is nothing more than appetite. It is the subject of which they partake that makes the difference between cannibals and people: some persons are curious to watch hangings, other persons are curious about ancient lands.

Curtain Raisers
Four men who raised the curtain masking the heart of man: Solomon, Socrates, Shakespeare, Spinoza.

Customs
Are man's symbolic gestures to perpetuate

his finest experiences in a world of fleeing time; the yearning for commemoration is the anguished urge to remain alive in the symbols of tradition.

Cynic
Means "dog" in Greek; the Greeks had the word for it.

A cynic is worse than a fool. The fool lacks insight but has faith; the cynic lacks both, though his cloak of impudence covers this emptiness.

:-:

A cynic cannot see from here to tomorrow.

:-:

Cynicism
Cynicism opens two alternatives: the one, in the original Greek interpretation: "It's a dog's world; let's just lie in the sun while the day lasts"; the other: "Let's live it up, as best we can master the alley."

D

Danger

Is an unpredictable guest: your loyal friend may be the innocent rock on which you stumble while your open enemy may cause your rise. Perhaps here lies the mystic meaning of "Love thine enemy."

Darkness

Is the cloth from which our little universe is spun. Away from the aura around this small globe, the spheres are bleak and cold. It is in us to reflect light and warmth; without us there is nothing.

Darwin

If Darwin had appeared on the scientific scene a hundred years later, he never would have considered European man the acme of evolution.

Day

A day is just a day, if even that. It is we who make it holi-, holy or hellish.

Daydreams

Are exciting only as long as they remain dreams.

The Dead

Let not the dead bury their dead; they might rise again.

Death

Perhaps our fear of death is but embryonic fear of life.

:-:

Death is a sideline guest who arrives and departs, but life comes to stay, with its thousand problems, difficulties and obstacles. It is life that deserves our concern and our fears, not death.

:-:

Some persons make such great efforts preparing themselves for life, as if they were to go on living for a thousand years. They are so busy getting ready that they hardly get to living.

:-:

You have laughed God out of your schools, out of your books, and out of your life, but you cannot laugh Him out of your death.

:-:

You still do your three score and ten, and then sink into dust knowing not the why and wherefore of this fleeting dream-trot in the arena of the human anthill.

:-:

It matters less when we die than how much of our life will live on.

:-:

Man sometimes lives, but constantly dies.

:-:

The thought of Life seldom occurs but at the time of death.

:-:

The fool dies only once.

:-:

It is not the fear of death that saddens people, but the love of life.

:-:

While we dream we think we are being real;

perhaps our reality is only a kind of dream, and death the awakening.

:-:

Death is a solemn reminder that life should be lived, not spent.

:-:

No man has nine lives but some die nine deaths.

:-:

Leave this world the way you found it: a heap of suffering and a drop of blessing. Don't run out without giving some of the latter—so many do.

:-:

Death is life's most persuasive reminder, and yet there are so many who can't read the message of the skull.

:-:

No man who understands death will misunderstand life.

:-:

There may be no life in death-time; there is certainly too much of death in life-time.

:-:

So many plot to become gravediggers of

neighbor nations. The spade is patient; it will bury them all.

:-:

Death is too sudden a visitor in reality, but too rare a guest in our thoughts. Were he to visit man's mind more often, perhaps this would be a more somber but more gentle race.

:-:

Many a man whom life had treated shabbily, death raised to exalted heights—death, the silent arbiter over glory and oblivion.

:-:

Youth can experience death, but only age can experience dying.

:-:

Should come to us; we should not be delivered to it.

:-:

There have been priests bold enough to insinuate that Persephone had raised for them the veil of the underworld. I do not mind such blatant self-arrogation; I merely find distasteful the efforts of these boors claiming intimacy with divine subtlety.

:-:

Those who value life fear not death.

:-:

Life after death: there must be something better than that.

:-:

It was the custom among the ancient Hebrews to bend the thumb of the deceased so that the folded hand would read like the word "Shaddai"—"The Destroyer!" This was one of the many circumscribed ways of referring to the Almighty.

Death is the great destroyer and thus the great reminder: *Vanitas, vanitatum vanitas!*

:-:

Comes as often too late as it comes too early.

:-:

The sages ride from this world silently; the clowns wish for an exit with pomp and fanfare.

Decalogue

In the centuries before Ezra the Scribe rulers of Judea encouraged another ten instructions:

Do not enslave your fellow man.

Do not put yourself above your fellow man.

Do not injure the weak.

Do not submit to the evildoer.

Where there are strong, be on the side of the weak.

Judge not your neighbor by the shape of
his body or the beliefs of his soul.

Do not arrogate to yourself the law that
belongs to the people.

Respect the freedom of all and the privilege of none.

Bar none from the road to the top.

Be ever helpful and compassionate.

Deceit

Is like a rose; it smells sweetest when it is
about to rot.

:-:

No one deceives us more often than we do
ourselves.

Decision

In most people is little more than awareness
of which way the winds of desire blow.

Deeds

Are God's measure of man, but people still
use the Devil's currency of words, words, words,
words . . .

:-:

One good deed may not beget another, but
an evil deed will not beget a good one.

:-:

If man is the image of God, then his deeds certainly belie His features.

:-:

Deeds only matter in the final analysis. Some nations gave their all to build up the body, like the Spartans; others to develop the mind, like the Athenians. The Judeans, however, cultivated the God-bound deed, *Mitzwah,* the act humane.

:-:

Better that your words follow you than run ahead of you.

Defeat
Can be fate's kindest admonition.

Deicide
With all the sounds and fanfare of the Vatican Council gone, for the Jews the old sad position remained: the vicious charge of deicide.

The Christian Churches and schools continue to narrate the hate born fable of the Jew as killer of God.

The Christians want us to forget and forgive them their unrelenting teaching of anti-Semitism and the resulting pogroms and massacres, but they desire to retain in their canon and catechism the pernicious legend of the Jew as crucifier.

:-:

What a silly word! How can man kill God? Is God dead?

If he is still alive, how stands up the vindictive murder charge against a whole people?

Delay

In judgment is a victory for reason.

Demagogue

The sanctimonious voice of righteousness is standard with the demagogue. No sincere man has as honest a face as the professional confidence man.

:-:

All tyrannical and demagogic undoings have their motivations. In fact, in this motivation lies the root of the evil.

:-:

The small ones fool the people; the big ones themselves too.

Demigods

Judaism bars the crown of divinity from all and everything but the *Ruach Hakodesh*—the Holy Spirit—that is the One Eternal, the *Echod*.

It places the crown upon the Torah, the knowledge of God, the indwelling of God in man; God alone is King.

Democracy

With corruption is better than tyranny without it.

:-:

Democracy in its inherent toleration must be on guard against self-destruction.

:-:

The world has for so many thousands of years been accustomed to be ruled by despots that even in democracies people still seek out overbearing men. At the helm they want a captain with a flourish.

:-:

The laws operate under a Constitution that guarantees all citizens freedom in the pursuit of their happiness, but they will more often than not fail to recognize a crime committed against a black man by a member of the sallow race which euphemistically refers to itself as white. And the schools—yes indeed, the schools—they teach democracy, but strictly beyond our own country. They teach biology, but somehow, on every page of text by gentleman's agreement there is a silent exclusion clause, and it is that segregative aside which dominates their pedagogy, not the verity of the official sciences.

In our own blessed South, Christ stops at the doorstep, the law protects the criminal and not the victim, and the school teaches a unity it doesn't believe in and practices a separation which it doesn't teach.

It seems that a good part of the world lives within a false and pretentious maze which shuts out the great truths beyond. Isn't it time we left this façade-trap and started living life all over again from real people to real people instead of from graven image to graven image?

Desire

Is given to all, discrimination to few.

:-:

Desire is the appetite of the soul; it is not eating that makes for illness but poor diet.

:-:

Desire alone can master desire. Ethics is a change of direction, not a change of nature.

:-:

It is easy to master desires that are tepid to begin with.

96 |

Despair

Is the mother of genius.

Despotism

Those who crave power have always held in contempt those who crave food.

Despots

. . . and other aggressors have no more precious ally than the dyed-in-the-wool pacifist who in the face of terror loses not only heart but also all sense of discretion.

:-:

The despot will identify himself with the State and then succeed in becoming its most ardent patriot.

Destiny

The vine dreams of climbing to the heavens —a twist in the wind and all is over.

:-:

They speak of glory, but settle for notoriety.

:-:

While they wait for it, the world runs away.

Devil

One may praise the Lord and serve the Devil.

:-:

The worst thing about the Devil is that most people flatly deny his existence. Obviously he can thus do considerable damage to body and soul without ever being blamed.

:-:

Devils must be running regular schools; there are so many people about of distinctly professional malevolence.

:-:

Every epoch in human history has its own gods and has its own devils. They keep changing and, of course, they all travel in different disguises. The Devil may journey about in a monk's habit; the messenger of the good Lord in a fancy shako and sash.

:-:

The devils of today wear a different masquerade from those of yestercentury. The devils of today wear a muddy and unadorned Marshal's uniform, or a peasant's tunic, covering their heads with a worker's cap and speaking softly with a worker's inflection. But beneath the artful grimace and gesticulation, to the experienced eye are clearly visible Satan's fleshless fingers and horse-hooved left foot.

Diaspora

Dispersion of the Jews all over the Mediterranean Basin and the Middle East began almost a thousand years before the Crucifixion and ended at the time of the Bar Kochba revolt in the middle of the second century of our era when a great Messiah perished at the hands of the Romans together with a half-million Hebrew rebels.

The Christians have made it a historiographic canon that God send Titus to disperse the Jews as punishment for the Crucifixion. Well, the Romans destroyed Jerusalem, as they destroyed Alexandria, Athens, Carthage, Syracuse, Corinth and a score of other cities. This was their way of ruling decapitalized countries. To say this was God's way is sheer blasphemy.

God does not throw thousands of Jewish infants from the walls of conquered Jerusalem; God does not garrote captured Jewish officers passing the Roman triumphal arch; God does not sell Jewish virgins in the slave markets on the Tiber.

And if this were God's will carried out by the

armies of Titus, then we must assume that the bloody Caesars of Rome from Gaius to Nero, in all their insane perversity, were not mere orgiastic marauders but the very arm of the Lord meting out justice.

Dictators

Have always adopted some kind of noble ideology as their surname.

Die

The man who will not die for anything has lived for nothing.

Difficulties

The Devil placed a thousand hurdles across the road to happiness, but man alone is still master of the mutual handicap.

Dignity

Takes a lifetime to acquire and a second to lose.

:-:

Dignity can be sold but not bought.

:-:

Dignity of the human person is the most meritorious aspect of democracy.

:-:

Dignity is a man-made respite of silence in a cacophonic world of affront and fury.

:-:

Dignity of man is the tyrant's most serious obstacle—hence his appalling efforts to destroy it.

Diplomacy
Is the verbal technique of saying what you don't mean and making it mean what you don't say.

:-:

Diplomacy is a game of make-believe with malice aforethought.

:-:

Sometimes it is better not to hit the nail on the head.

Disappointment
Is a signpost to true values.

Discontent
Has fired both holy vessels and unholy crackpots.

:-:

Discontent may become either spur or spite.

Discretion
Is the tact not to see what can't be helped.

Discussions
Professionals here are as distasteful as in cards or sports.

Disease
Can be conquered but hate has to be dissuaded.

Dissension
Is disagreeable but it is hate that is the danger.

Docility
Is one of the major social crimes cultivated in the average man and woman.

Doctrinaires
Have more often offended the heavens with their deeds than unbelievers with their heresies.

Dogma
The nature of life and death has forever beriddled the human mind. They have inspired a score of mythological fables. It is too bad that so often dull church people in their lack of

sense for the legendary have twisted the beau-
teous allegories into unsavory dogmas.

Donor
    The greatest gift is the art of giving.

                    :-:

    Those who give quietly, give twice.

Double Life
    We all lead it, only it is usually more
multiple.

Double Loyalty
    Is often challenged by those who have none.

Doubt
    Is the space for thought to feed; but no mind
can grow on space alone.

                    :-:

    Doubt is also a creed.

                    :-:

    It is amazing how some skeptics in one subject
become gullible approaching another.

Dreams
    Some set themselves the task of putting

dreams on the operating table; never were nightmares as lusty, reckless and fantastic as some peripatetic daydreams.

:-:

Dreams may betray our instincts but daylight displays them.

:-:

Dreams hide no secrets of which mind awake is unaware.

:-:

What mysteries do the Philistines expect to find in their dream life if their real one is but commonplace?

Dueling
For a cause or trifle grew from the sport of men to the sport of nations.

Duty
Duty is a virtue, but charity is the word of God.

E

Eating

Some fret about food as if salvation lay hidden in a vegetable.

Economics

Have hardly changed the people, but people have changed economy.

:-:

Man, so imperfect in body and mind, demands perfection of all things in his social and economic structure.

Economy

He who skimps on the seed will raise a poor harvest.

Education

Will eliminate foolishness but not deviltry.

:-:

God has been separated from our schools;

that may be all right, but the Devil was left there and that is not fair. The Devil of prejudice, arrogance, hatred, envy, home-grown superstition, and success-greed hovers over the school benches. You can't exorcise the Devil by looking the other way.

:-:

Education in conscientious living will change the face of mankind; knowledge alone will only reshape the grimace.

:-:

Perhaps one could teach goodness as one teaches algebra—or is there no logic to kindness?

:-:

The thinking of people usually depends upon which side of their bread is buttered. This is especially true of the thinking done by the teaching profession in countries where the state administration does all the buttering.

:-:

A man may be as smart as a book, and just as heartless.

:-:

One need not be learned in the head to do the right thing, but rather learned in the heart.

The learning of the heart is the most neglected branch of education today. The schools leave it to the churches and the churches leave it to the home, and how many homes are the proper place for character education?

:-:

The heart can learn only from another heart. The printed word does not teach it.

:-:

Education is in no way an indicator of moral responsibility; the intelligentsia of Germany avowedly supported Hitler, those of Russia supported Stalin and those of China support Mao, yet each of these dictators, by self-admission as well as irrefutable evidence, stands convicted as a mass murderer.

:-:

The system provides for instruction in almost any field excepting human conduct. In some schools they even teach you how to use a camera and how to collect stamps, but how to live a free man's life is left to latchkey parents and the older gang around the block. They have bolted the front gate against God and religion, but the Devil sneaks in through the back door.

:-:

What is wrong with education that makes 100 million Germans cheer Hitler; or 200 million Russians mummify Stalin so that the next thousand years may behold him; or 600 million Chinese bow daily before Mao's picture; or fifty million Italians hail Mussolini's forked tongue? And, finally, what's wrong with education in some segments of our own country where men will invite a manure-sniffing dog to sleep on their cot and women will place an evil-smelling cat on their bed pillow, but none would permit a colored man to live in the same block or eat at the same counter?

:-:

God needs no man in His perfection, but man needs God, or life becomes a mere drifting amidst the debris of everyday existence. What good is acquainting the pupil with this or the other detail of his surroundings: letting him know a bit about botany and zoology, a bit about geography and history, how to write and how to read, how to look up nature through its simple laws of physics, and even how to measure distances among a thousand huge rocks whirling through space? What good are these bits of information if the pupil receives no guidance as to how to be a better man among a better people.

:-:

We have said it before, and we say it again—the educated person is not a better person because of his or her knowledge, but only a more dangerous one.

The most educated nations, the Caesarean Romans, the Hitlerian Germans, or the Stalinist Russians have the most revolting deeds on their conscience, or where the conscience should be.

It is conscience that distinguishes good men from evil, and not an array of facts stored up in the brain. And it is lack of conscience that accounts for the fundamental failure of educational systems in the West as well as in the East.

Out of the 100,000 physicians of Hitler's Germany the records fail to show a single member protesting against the horrid vivisections perpetrated on forcibly hospitalized Jews.

:-:

The doctor who practices in a hospital that refuses to bind a Negro's wound; the clergyman who pontificates from a pulpit that never faces a Negro; the teacher who writes on a blackboard "For Whites Only"; the physicist employed in a laboratory in which the colored man is a synonym for porter; the judge, who in a case of a non-white plaintiff or defendant, becomes, by a flip of his hand toward a malevolent jury, midwife to a miscarriage of justice—all those scientists, clergymen and other educated people are a devastating argument against any contention that learning of the kind that is being dished out in the Western and Eastern world alike has brought about, or will bring about, betterment of mankind.

:-:

As long as educational blueprints are drafted on a foundation of success instead of citizenship and humanship they will never produce more than smart professionals.

:-:

If you wish to acquaint yourself with the deficiencies of our educational systems, look not at the schools or the pupils, but at the adults. Our teaching made them what they are. Find out what's wrong with our adults and you'll get at what's wrong with our pedagogy.

Ego
Reason is never without the current of the ego and the wind of desire. No ship ever sailed the oceans without water and wind. No man

110 |

ever went through life not borne and driven by the two classical passions of Self and the great Wish.

Egocentricity
Selflessness is the highest form of selfishness.

Egotism
The most difficult person to make friends with is yourself.

:-:

Virtue is not inborn in man, but egotism is.

Eloquence
Is these days a weapon, not a virtue.

Emancipation
Of world womanhood is still to come. Ninety per cent of them are still bound by social and caste structure to lowly kitchen duty, which some day in the future will be taken over by automation.

Emotions
If we only had a mirror for the soul, we would prepare our mind and adjust our emotions before we faced people.

Empathy

Those who say they feel for all, likely feel only for one, their very own one.

Encyclopedists

Cumulative erudition is more appropriate on a shelf than in a man.

Enemies

Are not those who hate us, but rather those whom we hate.

:-:

The just never love their enemies; they would otherwise strengthen injustice.

:-:

Hate your enemies, but make certain they are also enemies of mankind.

:-:

Feed not the rattler with the milk of kindness lest the vipers grow bold and poison your neighbor.

The Enemy

The character of mankind's foe changes from epoch to epoch. In earliest times anarchy was the great threat, the refusal of individual or tribe to respect the privileges of others. Pretentious usurpers were later the archfoes. Even religion for a while became a threat as suppressive organization. At present it is pretentious social welfare, sailing under the red flag of Communism, threatening to engulf mankind with a tyrannical net spread by cunning demagogues.

Enemy Love

Only dogs lick the hand that beats them.

Epigoni

Often appropriate the laurels that should adorn the originator.

Equality

The Marxist system, on a platform of "no one with power over others," has created a spectacular One with power over all.

:-:

Calling all citizens "comrades" may make some of them feel equal, but one glance from the boots of the peasant to those of the party leader will tell the difference.

:-:

All men are not equal, but their rights are.

:-:

All men are equal in sin, unequal in virtue.

:-:

Equality before the law is often injustice before reality: to fine the rich the same amount as the poor works hardship on the poor, none on the affluent.

Equanimity

Is sometimes a symptom of indifference and not of mastered emotions.

Equivocation

Some men refuse to take a position and avoid even the expression of an attitude. Equivocation is frustrating and dull. The ancient Hebrews called them "men without salt."

Error

The errors of today are still veiled; those of yesterday are an open book.

:-:

Knowledge is frequently not truth but a lesser error.

:-:

The great may go wrong, but they do not try to cover their tracks.

Established

Nothing is more difficult to eradicate than established stupidity.

Eternal Light

Some of its caretakers imagine they are the harbingers of the Flame.

Eternity

It is beyond man's pale where time begins.

Ethereal

Even into the darkest soul passes, at least once in life, a ray of awareness of the supernatural, sometimes at the birth of a child or the death of a soul. Like to those living in ancient Egypt's *Amenti,* the land of the dead, through which passed once a day the sun god, Ra.

Ethics

Man's study of nature will not improve his conduct; man's study of himself might.

:-:

Physicists have improved the tempo of man but not his temper.

:-:

If man would spend as much time on his soul as he does on his car, we would all fare better.

:-:

People live on different wavelengths of time. Some live for the hour, others for the months or years, but few only for eternity. Long-range living is the way of true ethics.

:-:

If you failed to learn ethics at six, you will not learn it at eighty.

:-:

Those who wish to make public morals complicated desire not to uncover truth but to hide it.

:-:

Ethics does not consist in making yourself happy but rather in making this a happier world.

:-:

It is the devil's priesthood that puts themselves up as judges over the morals of men and women, making a virtue out of sexual impotence and frigidity and making a mockery of ethics.

Eugenics

The apple does not fall far from the tree, but what a difference between apple and apple.

Evil

There is so much misery and massacre in this world that to deny it one is either a fool or a faker.

:-:

The fact that we can never expect to eradicate evil does not imply that we should not incessantly fight it.

Evolution

The protoplasm may be at the foot of evolution; man certainly is not its crown.

:-:

We assume that only the fittest of each species survived, yet we find ourselves surrounded by multitudes of unfit creatures.

:-:

Hate must be the highest form of emotion. We encounter so much of it now that we seem to stand on a peak of evolutionary progress.

:-:

The neat classification of animal life into higher and lower forms is like the Social Register: it is all right with the people listed in it but hardly a proper guide for the Lord.

:-:

The world has shifted in the last ten thousand years from an era of bestial primitives to one of highly educated beasts.

:-:

I do not like to make unkind references to Professors Darwin, Wallace and their predecessors, but I have a suspicion it may just be possible that the goats have readied their own scale of evolution in which of course they are way on top and biologists may be way at the bottom.

:-:

But all this is mere talk anyhow, so what does it matter who claims to be king of the jungle? For all we know, this our mossy globe, this speck of flying dust particle may be just that in the eyes of the good Lord and we may never get to know the immense universe or multiverse.

Some college teachers have proclaimed us the peak.

I sometimes wonder if the infinite and eternal Essence is aware that this tiny speck of dirt is around.

:-:

History proves that the stronger best the weaker, not that the better win over the sinister.

Experience

If the dead were to rise and bury the living, I doubt if they'd make a better world. The only thing man seems to learn from experience is that it bears repetition. They killed the Czar to end tyranny, and began a free state with a new tyrant.

Exploiters

To understand the exploiters and dictators of today it is essential to know those of the past.

Explorers

The mission of the conquistadors was not to bring the teachings of Christ to the pagans, but to bring gold to the Christian kings, and where there was no gold, to bring the pagans themselves and beat gold out of their freedom.

The Catholic kings of Spain and Portugal, like the Protestant kings and queens of England, had one mission only, and that was one, not of giving, but taking. Where they could not haul gold or silver or furs, they hauled slaves and slaves again.

Exploration, to the princely heads of Renaissance Europe, was not a romantic adventure of enjoying new lands and new people, and the goodness of free intercourse in commerce, in culture and conventions. Discovery to them, meant finding out where the gold and silver were kept, and where the natives could be trapped like beasts in dugouts or foxes in forests. There was not even honor among thieves, for when the Spanish and Portuguese had laid their privateering hands on the properties of the Africans and American Indians, Elizabeth, the queen of the pirates, sent her men-of-war to rob the plunderers.

Eyes

Can as well conceal a betrayal as betray what they conceal.

F

Faa-Fil-Lah

The Moslem saint's nirvana or annihilation in God is as little an ethical act as the ascetic seclusion of the Christian Trappist. An act exists as ethical or unethical only in relation to others. A flight into mystical hermitage may bring one peace or serenity or forgetfulness but never is it a matter of morals. The saint is often more selfish than the sinner. Running away from the cares and battles of life may serve the interests of a burdened soul, but in the light of social morality it is just another deed strictly for the sake of the benefits it offers the doer.

Facts

Are difficult to accept because they must be grasped; fancies are quickly taken on, since they require belief only.

Faddists

Use the reasoning of a scholar to prove a proposition little removed from old wives' fairy tales.

Failure

If you can do nothing with yourself, others are not likely to do better.

Failures

Do not teach unless they are understood.

Fairy Tales

The great tales were never written for the young. But our time has lost the spiritual naïveté of life, so only the children are left to respond to the significance of the ancient lore.

:-:

Are shot through with ancient adult horror stories that dominated the primitive Teutons and Mongols: Man-eating monsters, dragons, wolves and vampires. It is time to give these "fairy tales" back to primordial man and add to the little of true children's literature we already possess.

Faith

There is no short cut to true faith; yet so

many drop out into the easy byways of superstition and false beliefs.

:-:

Faith will not waver where reason is its foundation.

:-:

Faith fundamentally is given only to those who take the road of reason to the bitter end.

:-:

Faith is nothing but knowledge that what we understand is only a shadow of the Unknown. Faith is the science of the pitiful limitations of man's mental scope.

:-:

Faith has its weaknesses, but faithlessness is the poorest substitute.

:-:

Adonai Echod! God is One, and the One lives in the heart of man, and the love to God and the love to man are one and the same. This is not only the beginning of true faith, this is all of it; the rest is silence.

:-:

The man who has his own religion has a fool for a priest.

:-:

Faith is belief in the invisible. It would be a dull world, indeed, if only the visible were reality.

:-:

Faith and doubt are brothers under the skin.

:-:

Faith is not proven by the number of believers. Abraham was alone and he had the truth against a whole generation of pagans.

:-:

Faith must transcend the narrowness of limited God given only to this, man's little world, and rise to adoration of *Elohim,* the God of Eternities, the Lord of infinite Universes.

:-:

The question in our sophisticated time is not what your faith is, but rather how valid have you made your faith.

Fame
Its seekers show that strange preference for notoriety among the many to appreciation by the few.

:-:

The "No" of one expert outweighs the "Yes" of a thousand amateurs.

:-:

Fame runs in circles. One can be burning with ambition within his little circle and be cold to the rest of the world.

:-:

Fame spreads, elusive in the grasping arms of turbulent man until all the strength and time and breath inherent to mortals are spent in the embrace of the clothed chimera, and man is left nothing but a stumbling shadow of his true self.

:-:

Fame cannot be possessed. It cannot even be arrested, and if some of the naively ambitious hold it for their own, let them take only one further look to find how precarious is their grasp.

:-:

Wait a thousand years before you cast a man in bronze and put him on a pedestal; you may find your hero was not carrying the torch of freedom, but just lighting a comfortable hearth for himself.

Familiarity

Purity is not disturbed by a closer look; pretense is.

Family

Relatives may become friends, but friends are always kin.

Fascism

The path of the dictator is paved with democratic pronouncements.

Fatalism

The man who hates his enemies is no wiser than the child who hits at the chair over which he has stumbled.

Fate

Caesar thought that he cast the dice of fate, but to the far heavens in distant night it was merely one hill of ants robbing another.

:-:

Fate holds this tiny globe in its giant palm, hardly taking note of the dust on it called man.

:-:

The unpredictable fall of events in our erratic stream of life. Sometimes what looks like a whirling trap to certain doom throws us onto a most attractive shore and what appears a stretch of gentle caressing waves will drag the unsuspecting to perdition. You cannot tell what this goddess spins until the web is done and carried by the winds to the far-blue rocks of posterity.

Faults

It is not the faults we have, but those we see in others that make us intolerable.

Fear

May be justified, but it will not bring justice.

:-:

Who has the fear of God never had His love.

:-:

Fear is the severest of pains, and the least alleviated.

:-:

The unknown fears trouble us most.

:-:

Fear means nursing a problem instead of facing it. It is a play of self-pity ignoring the in-

evitable. It takes courage to brush aside brood-
ings of temerity. Our sages said that the courageous die by the blade, the timid by a thousand
strokes of their fears.

:-:

Those who endanger the safety of a state by
their urge for power are prone to panic the
people into fear of an imaginary enemy abroad.

:-:

The face of the courageous is chalked with
dread; it is only the reckless who know no
anxiety.

:-:

Some of the rich pay for having their minds
diverted by analysts from fears to which the
whole of the less affluent world is likewise subjected. The earth is full of fears beyond those
pampered few; the task is not to shield the pri-
vileged, but to rise against all that is oppressive.

:-:

Fears are not to be alleviated by hiring professional pacifiers, but eliminated by opposing
the men or institutions that create them.

Fearlessness
Is shown not so much by those who stoically

accept an inevitable verdict of death, but rather by those who could escape the death penalty if they would only submit.

Feeling

Perhaps the Cabbalist was right when he said: Feelings slumber in the throat; the weighty ones sink to the heart and the light ones fly out through the tongue.

Fellowship

You are what you arouse in fellow man.

:-:

Man cannot place himself outside the pale of fellowship. A drop disintegrates outside the waters. Man can be a god to man, and man can be a devil to man, but man without fellowship has neither meaning nor purpose.

Fellow-Travelers

They are so eager for perfection in social order that they accept chaos as a substitute provided it holds forth a promise for tomorrow.

Fence Sitters

Some fence sitters never cheer, always jeer—preferably their own team.

Fighting

Those who refuse to fight oppression are theologically uninformed if they base their decision on a Gospel quote, are thoroughly indolent if they point to the ubiquity of wars in history, and plain frightened if they tremble at the possibility of having their skins cut.

Flag

The American flag is a symbol, not of the nation, but of its freedom.

Flattery

Flattery is the first step on the road to slander.

:-:

Flattery is like an ill wind; it shifts without pause.

:-:

Men who tolerate flattery will never accept criticism.

:-:

Flattery is a scheme of the sly to bribe real people with make-believe currency.

:-:

The tongue that flatters is the tongue that poisons.

:-:

In the order of hate derision follows flattery.

:-:

The man who flatters is the man who libels.

Flight
Man still has failed to gain the secrets of muscle-powered bird flight although he has mastered the winds; just as he has conquered the waters by use of the boat, but not learned to swim like the fish.

Flowers
Petals that light up a feeling of beauty in one nation are just feed in another.

Foe
There is no better friend than a frank enemy.

Folly
One man's folly is the other man's faith.

Fools
Are not those who know little but rather those who know too much of what just isn't so.

:-:

Men are fools, but not so much as those who think themselves exceptions to this dictum.

Force

Has made slaves of men but it is courage that makes men of slaves.

Foreign Language

It's knowing a people's troubles and hopes that brings one close to them, not the speaking of their tongue.

:-:

With the number of platitudes and irrelevancies being spouted by mouth and pen in any one language, the acquisition of additional tongues should be soundly discouraged.

Foresight

Improve your hindsight and you will gain in foresight.

Forgetting

The art of forgetting is as important as that of remembering.

Forgiveness

Is an act of grace to the aggrieved, not the aggressor.

:-:

It is easy to forgive crimes perpetrated on others.

:-:

Forgive the criminal, forget not the crime.

:-:

The infant and the dying show the look of forgiveness—Eternity smiling at man's pitiful self-importance in coming and going.

:-:

Forgiveness is a decision no longer to see the evil; forgetfulness is understanding it as a part of the chain of woe.

:-:

Can you forgive the snake its poisonous fangs, the tarantula its sting, the leopard its claws? Such is man to man.

:-:

If it's divine to forgive, it's manly to forget.
The indolent forgive any crime so long as it is committed on others, and the churches are quite forgiving except when they themselves are attacked.
Pope Pius XII sent vehement protests to the Western leaders for bombarding Monte Cas-

sino, but not one, not a single one, for the massacring of millions of children, women and unarmed, chained men.

:-:

You may forgive your own enemy, but not the evildoers against others.

:-:

Maybe not I should ask forgiveness, but the good Lord Himself, should ask it for me.

Ask my forgiveness for having German Christians beat my poor old mother to death.

Ask my forgiveness for having German Christians shoot my four young cousins in front of their chained and bleeding parents.

Ask my forgiveness for having one million—I say it again, one million—children of my people marched to gas chambers by German Christians, where they choked to death, noxious fumes burning their little throats.

God owes us so much, so very much!

I cannot bless the heavenly hand that sent a Son to this world in whose name my people were bled to death.

And the end is not yet!

Fortune

Has no rhyme or reason, like the rock that

falls on an anthill. Perhaps the surviving ants think they were saved by divine providence and send up hymns of thanks.

:-:

Fortune, more than rarely, is great misfortune.

Free Men

Are bound by a thousand chains of conscience, love and duty; it is the slave to himself who stumbles through life unattached and careless, given to loose talk and loose thinking.

Freedom

Is the sole touchstone of social progress: a Communism that requires enslavement in order to gain freedom is like virtue predicated on crime.

:-:

Freedom lies not in the resignation to want, but rather in the accession to true values.

:-:

Freedom is not dominant where subjugation still exists, even in a corner.

:-:

Freedom knows only pro and contra with no neutrality in between.

:-:

When your grandfather or mine was a boy, even in America people were auctioned off on the same platform with grain and cattle. And our youth of the South went to school and passed by the shouting auctioneers haggling away human flesh, and they said nothing. This is the most vicious crime of them all, the crime of omission, of omitting to do something when faced with evil.

Where was the outcry against the peddling of human flesh? It wasn't there. What *was* there was the yell for the bloodhounds, with the whole town forming a posse to hunt down the poor black devil who ran away.

Where is the outcry of the youth of South Africa in our own days against the beating down of fellow men just because they want to be free or at least respected as men? The children of South Africa go to the same schools we do; they go to similar universities and colleges, and so did their parents. What is wrong that they are so silent?

What is wrong with education in our own South, in Red China, in the whole Soviet Empire, in South Africa, in the Arabic countries, where there are still over two million slaves in actual physical bondage? Why does youth remain silent, and by its silence, approve? Have they not learned right from wrong? Good from evil?

Of what value are all the bits of disjointed intelligence, bits of false history, bits of foreign languages, bits of art information, bits of falsified anthropology, pasted together with mathematics, physics, chemistry and biology? What kind of horrible harmony do they make, youthful personalities who seem to have snatched up a bit of everything except love for fellowman?

Friend

Wheat does not come without chaff. If you want your friend, accept his entourage.

:-:

One friend is worth a thousand acquaintances.

:-:

The worst enemies are those who were once your friends.

:-:

Many comrades are not bound by a unity of love but by a unity of hatred.

Friendship

Too often are relationships founded on dislike and envy called friendships, for we are bound to those we hate almost as much as to those we love. Perhaps hatred is an even stronger tie than affection; it is more lasting, and like love, seeks out its object, yearning to dwell in its shadow.

:-:

Like the Stone of Wisdom, friendship may be lying right in your backyard and you may never know it.

:-:

Those who cannot give friendship will rarely receive it and never hold it.

:-:

Your friend is the one who sees you as you would love to see yourself.

:-:

Friendship is a daydream beat of the heart for a face that lights it up. Only in dreams can one see in that simple trifle all virtues, valiance and varied attributes that warm the clasp of the hands. In the light of friendship, the commonplace fades into a serene glow and banality metamorphoses a romance. What touching reality in such dreams, and how barren existence in mere objective togetherness!

:-:

Meet with your friends in the core of the matter, where you agree, and not on the fringe where you differ.

:-:

Man's greatest gift to man is man.

Future

For a better tomorrow you have to better today.

:-:

The best way to look ahead is by looking back.

:-:

If you understand your past, the future will hold no riddles.

G

Gab

Some gabble with the tongue, others with the pen.

:-:

Every sinner was punished by the good Lord with a handicap: the dullard got the gift of gab.

Gambling

A gulp from the bitter brew of fear and hope to give some taste to a dull existence.

Generosity

To find fault in our heart is easy; to find generosity in it is difficult.

:-:

Generosity in the hands of the cunning is a weapon, not a virtue.

Genius

True genius is a servant of his cause, not its exploiter.

:-:

Genius is no part of madness, but madmen may have genius.

:-:

Three-quarters of the world's spiritual seedlings never hit the furrow of civilization. They perish before their time.

Germans

It is amazing how eager are the so-called better classes among the Germans to shove the Nazi decade into a forgotten past; these are the same German upper classes who placed before the world the curtain of their respectability behind which the unbelievable mass assassinations against the helpless were carried out.

Gifts

He who gives too much belittles the recipient.

Glory

Who pants after fame will sooner or later run out of breath.

:-:

The sweet smell of military victory has, like all perfumes, a very putrid matter as base.

:-:

The difference between gangsterism and imperialism is mainly in scale. The attacks of Hitler on Poland or Stalin on Finland, Alexander's plundering of Asia, Titus' sacking of Jerusalem or the banditry of the Vandals, the Vikings, the Normans, the Huns, the privateers of Queen Elizabeth, etc., etc.—it is only the size of these sanguinary excursions and the loot that distinguishes them from common holdups. Take off their gilded armor, fancy tunics, pretentious crowns and ludicrous rationalizations and before you stands a motley lot of bandits with tribal support.

Undraped of the purple, and marshal's shako, what we commonly teach and tell as history is only a series of criminal cases in which the victim is lampooned and the gunman glorified.

True history is yet to be written.

:-:

Every man in every nation likes to sail under the unfurling banner of some glorious slogan even if he carries a cargo of destruction and pestilence in his pirate hold.

142 |

Don't let the banner fool you. Let's board the ship and see what is under that shining deck.

God
Is not worried about His enemies, I feel, but some of His defenders are frightening to behold.

:-:

The essence of all Being is One, and there our wisdom ends. But this we feel and know as well as we, with our little souls, can grasp the thought: the way to God is man's love to man.

:-:

The soul of God is in the soul of man. There is no God but in the consciousness of innermost man.

:-:

God has no interpreters but man's hearkening, and the church may or may not speak His voice. The voice of God is too high for some to hear and too low for others, and it does not exist at all for the many, many who are deaf. The voice of God may speak through the morning green of a sun-kissed meadow, the melancholy rhymes of bittersweet poetry, the angry shouts of a dying soldier giving his life on the battlefield altar of freedom, the years of parental drudgery and filial sacrifice, heavenly sermons and songs leaving the lips of the truly inspired, the words of wisdom of sages then and now.

:-:

There is no God besides the God in the depths of man's mind. There is no love and inner freedom but that which springs from the fountain of true cognition. There is no unity but the everlasting truth borne by man's inner self.

:-:

Man lived without God for a million years. He now dwells in the presence of God, but does God dwell in the heart of man?

:-:

The ancient Hebrews did not write the name of God. I often wish the Christians would follow suit, as never was a word more misused in writing and speaking than the name of the Lord.

:-:

If modern man understands the Ways of the Lord, then the Master is in a bad way.

:-:

144 |

The small mind envisions a smallish God and then denies Him. One has to be a big man to see God in His glory, a very big man indeed.

:-:

The Hebrews have no name for Him, the Moslems have a hundred. Both suggest the same thing, that there are concepts as well as emotions that can be communicated only allegorically.

:-:

God is poor company for those who don't speak His language.

:-:

God moves in deepest silence over the sands, the oceans and the earth. Only the thirsty soul will spy His footprints.

:-:

God is a silent partner in this world, and man certainly gives Him the short end.

:-:

What we know of God we know from people, people speaking and people writing.

There is no other knowledge of God except by word of mouth and word of pen.

:-:

Nowhere does the name of God and justice appear more frequently than on the banner and the shield of the conqueror.

:-:

Man is left to his own devices, and the idea of an interfering and providential God is merely a figment of priestly imagination. If God can heal the sick, let Him heal all of them. If God can stop massacre, let Him stop all of it. If God can prevent starvation, let Him feed all the hungry.

Of one thing I am sure: wherever God is, He does not sit on a throne like a tyrant you can bribe with promises or sacrifices, be they goats, a barrel of wine or a good-sized chicken; a vow to refrain from drinking whiskey during Lent or a promise to hold to the diet at Ramadan will not affect His attitude toward His worshipers. If all the warring nations have their weapons blessed by the priests, I don't think the good Lord can hear any of them, and I am afraid all confessions remain right there with the priests in the box. You don't really think the good Lord has an ear for all the self-confessed sins or the billion little people who get on their knees for relief. Perhaps confessing little sins is good for the soul, but the big crimes that are bad for humanity go on and on. No divine power intervened when whole nations were obliterated, when whole cities were put to the torch, when whole continents were enslaved.

This world is not God's domain, not a God to whom you can pray like a subservient peasant before his cruel master.

There is but one God. He is the conscience in your heart. The Hebrews called it Shechinah; it is the indwelling of divinity in man. There is no God on the outside, neither on Olympus nor in the Himalayas nor anywhere above the clouds, nor is there any hell below except rock and water and again rock and fire.

If you have never heard the voice of God within you, you shall never hear the voice of God outside of you, and all those who have claimed to have heard the voice from the outside were either dreamers or schemers.

:-:

Praising God is fallacious. If perchance He is the kind praise would please, He is not much of a God, and if—as I think—He is oblivious of it, then wherefore the praise?

:-:

What we know of God we know from people, people speaking and people writing.

Religion is but a matter of scroll and parchment, and the reason why one man identifies God with Mohammed while across the broad river his neighbor identifies Him through Laotse is purely a matter of their using different libraries.

People can live in the same building and still be of different faith. Whatever book or bible dominates the desk, that is the religion of the house; as whatever law dominated a province in post-medieval Germany or in medieval India became the religion of the province. That is why you have Protestants in Prussia and Catholics across the river in Bavaria.

God never wrote in books, nor did His son. From the way in which so many people in the Western World regard God, one must assume He was a Jew who spoke Hebrew only, although some Scriptures are written in Aramaic. But what of the rest of the world? Most people in India and China and South Asian countries do not even know there is a Hebrew language; still they revere scriptures and other messages of God.

In my eyes it shows rather short-sighted thinking to attribute to the good Lord only such very recent religious documents as those available in the early antiquity of Eurasia. I have always resented the idea of degrading the good Lord to the rank of an editor of priestly documents.

:-:

God takes giant steps; He is not even aware of what takes place under His boots.

:-:

God proposes, but man knows different. That's why this world is not God's world.

:-:

A God who permits the gassing of a million children and five million unarmed adults by human hyenas may be a Teutonic deity but certainly not the God of Love.

:-:

The world is a stage and God is in the audience.

Godhead
To get nearer to God, come closer to man.

Golden Mean
Those who follow the golden middle way often have a profound appreciation of the value of gold.

Golden Rule

Do unto others as you say you do.

Golgotha

The drama of Golgotha fades away before the grim religious and secular punishments meted out to millions of persons in the course of history.

What makes Jesus of the New Testament different is not his suffering—millions have suffered more, much more, for less, indeed for nothing—as, for instance, the Jews in Auschwitz. The story of Jesus, like the story of Socrates or Thomas More, is the tale of a man who wished death in order to carry out a self-imposed task, Jesus to uphold humility, Socrates to uphold freedom and More to uphold virtue.

They all could have escaped their ultimate fate; they chose death so their idea might live.

In a way, Jesus, Socrates and More were spiritual suicides. Their lives were in their hands; they could have lived but for a single word. They did not want to say it. Their martyrdom was self-imposed for the greater glory of their calling.

History has many men who died for a cause. If not for these men, life would hardly be worth living.

Good Book

Where is the clergy when the barricades are up? Where is the clergy when pressure hose and shot are directed against a suppressed minority?

They are kneeling in prayer at the altar? They are reading the Good Book?

No book is good when it keeps a man from freedom's struggle and no prayer is worth saying that keeps a man from cursing the Devil, out loud and to his face. Silence is the Devil's tongue when the world cries out.

Good Cheer

Is not virtue but a step toward it. Baal Shem-Tov, the Hebrew mystic, said: "I can sing a prayer as well as say it."

Good Government

Good government is where the average citizen can take on the function of parliamentary representative or even prime minister. A country that requires as governors men of steel will wind up with men of bayonets.

Good Times

Some people bear up worse under good times than under bad.

Goodness

Is held in such low regard it takes courage to profess it.

:-:

No rite or ritual is essential, but goodness is.

Gospels

Not a shred or tile or stone of evidence has turned up in the last twenty years of intensified excavations in Palestine to confirm by contemporary evidence the tragic drama of the Golgotha executions. Thousands of documents have been unearthed and uncaved, adding knowledge and verification to the Bible and its people. No such has been found relating to Gospel history.

As long as the Christian churches continue teaching as history a Vatican-propagated Greek version of a fourth-century biographical horror tale as to how the Jews maliciously murdered a Nazarene carpenter who was God in the flesh —as long as this biased drama exists, that makes the Jew the father of sin and its hereditary devilish master—there will continue to be, as there has been in the Western world, a realm of Jew hatred.

The great massacres of Jews, from the Visigoths to Hitler and from the Crusaders to the

Ukraine, can be laid directly at the feet of Christian theology about the Crucifixion.

The Jew must be burned—and if not this, then scourged—and if not this, ostracized.

No Christian country is so small, no church so modest, that it fails to instill in its flock and children the gospel of God's willful and savage murder at Jewish hands. Anti-Semitism is daily reborn with every sermon in Christology. It will not cease until such bloody theology has ended.

Gossip

We need not know a man's personal follies to understand his philosophy.

Government

By observation is the so-called People's Democracy. The citizens are apprised of various governmental changes or edicts; they don't have any part in making them, they are merely observers!

:-:

Tyrants have often ruled in the name of the people; democracy, however, is based on the people ruling themselves.

:-:

Government where there is no opposition cannot be a people's government.

Grading

That we have great men in our time and recent times is not because of our educational system, but rather in spite of it. They are the ones the teachers couldn't spoil. At least they couldn't spoil them altogether, although some important figures of our times bear the mark of moral confusion and anti-social behavior. Some of them use their gifts and talents to sing the praise of totalitarian dictators. Others do not hesitate to undermine and betray the welfare of the democratic community they live in.

How can it be otherwise in a society in which the teachers have not yet learned that youth raised in ambition, self-assertion and competitive avarice will not grow into charitable adulthood. And if some think that they can beat more knowledge into youth by the scourge of the contest than by mere teaching, I would say that an ounce of human kindness is worth a ton of so-called knowledge. It isn't that you need the scourge to train the youth, just as it isn't the whip you need to keep man at work. Give a man a proper job and a proper wage and freedom to live in, and he will stay at a task until it is done, because man is made to work. And give a child answers to his curious mind in open manner and in proper time, and give him freedom to participate in equal manner with all his classmates without fear of being degraded, without bribe of rank promises, and the child will follow your teaching eagerly, because youth wants to learn.

Does a father grade his children? Does he mark them low and high, passing and failing? They are his to teach and love alike. And if teachers lack the color of speech or the power of persuasion to entertain the interests of the young, perhaps they should seek for other fields of work instead of holding school over a herd of uneasy scholars, and leave teaching to those who feel the calling and have the cordiality of the teaching mind.

Gradualization

The Southern abolitionists wish to reduce racial injustices inch by inch. They claim a sudden, total flare of freedom in their states might hurt the sensitivities of the indigenous natives.

Grammar

The best grammarian still can't write a verse.

:-:

Grammarians make no new thoughts, but thoughts make new grammar.

Grandparents

Are the lost branch of this generation; the offspring does not rightly know where to place them on the family tree.

Gratitude

Such is the soil of man's heart that you may plant the sweetest seed and harvest stone.

:-:

People who set out to hurt you will, in the long run, help you as often as those who desire to be of assistance may harm you.

:-:

Gratitude forever faces the obstacle of envy.

Grave

The real hero dies a silent death and lies in an unmarked grave.

:-:

If the epitaphs were but half true, this were the best of worlds.

Great Books

Are not those that were important in past centuries but those of contemporary impact.

Great Ideas

Were never discovered by one man, but often halted by one.

Great Thoughts

Ever walk the open road. Pretenses seek out the unclear byways.

Greatness

There are great stages in a little man's life and small moments in the life of the great.

:-:

Big people are sometimes small men and little people are often really big.

:-:

Greatness lies less in the skill to succeed than in the ability to accede.

:-:

Raising yourself is a skill, raising your fellow man is a virtue.

:-:

Great men are simple, but what intricate simplicity!

:-:

A man deserves the name "great" only if he left a heritage of benefaction to the people; if he enriched no one but himself, he was greedy, not great, no matter how gargantuan his appetite.

:-:

Great is not the man who has taken from life and from the people a thousandfold share. Great is the man who has given to life and to the people with never-ending perseverance.

Perhaps the greatest man of all is the man no one knows.

:-:

Perhaps the greatest minds never preached and never wrote; perhaps the greatest books were never published.

Grief

Can only be cured by reason, and reason rests with God.

:-:

Those who do not care easily master grief.

:-:

To suffer grief may be unavoidable; to inflict it is not.

:-:

Grief need not last to prove its profundity; one can trespass inferno in one short night.

Guest
Ask yourself sometime, how would you find yourself, as a guest, a neighbor or a competitor?

Guilt
The feeling of guilt is the gateway to virtue.

:-:

Man is equal to any crime or sin under given circumstances. Those whom fate spared or favored are inclined to condemn in haste the one who drew a bad lot.

:-:

Guilt by association is not conclusive, but considerable. I think little of the virgin who spends her days in a brothel.

:-:

Some of the most unspeakable crimes leave telling marks but no telling evidence.

:-:

Lack of punishment is no proof of innocence.

Hachukkim

Some of the laws of the Torah cannot be rationally justified. Perhaps some of them had only one purpose, to make all the people of the country do the same thing at the same time with the same devotion—a practice in discipline and religion, a training in unity and obedience to higher principles.

Hands

Beware of the grip that is too firm; it may be calculated.

Happiness

Is no criterion for either health or wisdom; the foul and the fool can be happy as a drunken sow.

:-:

Happiness to be true must be oriented on

landmarks much greater than one's own little personal joys and gratifications.

:-:

Perhaps hogs are happy, but man should be moved by a greater wish than to be jolly.

:-:

Happiness is not a virtue, but virtue brings happiness.

:-:

Happiness is determined by the number of people one loves.

:-:

Happiness is a task, not a gift.

:-:

Don't try to make people happy; just avoid making them unhappy.

Harmony

I wonder if a harmonious personality is a sign of great wisdom or perhaps only of incalculable indifference.

Haste

Those who run through life will get there quickly, but hardly well-composed.

Hate

Dictators long ago found out it is easier to unite people in common hatred than in common love.

:-:

Hate binds no less than love. The free man will want to put it behind him. Hatred disfigures your lips no less than your words.

:-:

One who hates an evildoer fails to recognize that those with ill will, more often than not, serve us instead of their own interests.

:-:

One may avoid, confine or punish a culprit without snarling. To love an enemy, however, is absurd; it is difficult enough to love one's friends.

:-:

Whatever you love, you are its master; whatever you hate, you are its slave.

:-:

Hate ignores the wise truth that all evildoers are such by necessity. They do need to be curbed, like thorns or thistles, but in weeding hate is unwarranted.

:-:

Do not aspire to love your enemies, but endeavor to deal justly with those you hate.

:-:

Nothing is easier to teach than hate; that is perhaps the reason why tyrants invariably find someone or something for their people to hate. With this hatred they unite them; with this hatred they hold them—it comes easy to man.

:-:

It takes a heroic heart and deep insight to pull one's mind out of the mire of hate pattern. Hate has great fascination. *To nothing does man veer more readily than to hate.* The tyrant knows what the people do not suspect: that hate is the greatest unifier. Hate always marks the beginning of tyranny. Make the people hate a common enemy and they will forget everything and everyone else.

Hate has been the secret weapon of dictators since time began. All ideologies of all reformers mean nothing if hate is the common bond of their pattern of life. No arguments will win out against *raisonnement* born of hate.

:-:

Tell me what you hate and I will tell you what you are.

Heart
Is the mind's bridge to wisdom.

:-:

The world is full of ailing hearts; quacks abound and rare is the doctor.

Heaven
The Cabbalah speaks of ten steps to heaven. There is modesty, and courage, and devotion, and so on. The book never mentions libido as a rung to beatitude.

The Heavens
Are not the seat of God but a reminder of His unseen Presence.

Hell
Cannot outdo mankind's own mutual bestiality.

:-:

Some theologians appear to think one must live like hell in this world to avoid it in the other.

Help
The man who needs no one's help is a lonely man indeed.

:-:

To help one has to learn, even as one has to learn how to harm; it is only indifference that comes to man naturally.

Heritage
You can tell a thousand years later when a great man left his imprint on the mind of a nation.

:-:

So many pride themselves upon their ancient heritage, but have yet to find out what their grandparents were like.

Hermit
The hermit is a dull man preoccupied with nothing but his little self, be it physical, be it spiritual. The wise man, like Socrates, seeks out the people of the world and makes them part of his own self, the greater Self of the greater man.

Hero Worship
Has an uncanny tendency to choose scoundrels as the object of adulation.

Heroes
Don't rise, they are raised.

:-:

True honor does not crave recognition, as true wisdom craves not publicity. The great heroes and the great men of wisdom walk silently through the bypaths of mankind.

:-:

Some of those buried in prison yards deserved mausoleums, and many of those entombed in cathedral sepulchers should have been thrown to the jackals. The tombstone tells when you died not how you lived.

Heroism

The hero is not a man without fear, but one who hates injustice more than he loves personal safety.

:-:

The man who will risk his life on a childish dare may not do the same if the welfare of a whole nation hangs on it.

:-:

Rare indeed is the hero who yearns not for medals of the day but for the final victory in a far distant tomorrow.

:-:

Some heroes are created by a fleeting moment;

nothing in their past or later life carries even a trace of heroism.

:-:

No one is so valorous that he was not once a coward.

Historians

The trouble with historians is they are invariably trying to sell something instead of just reporting.

:-:

Historians more often than not like to ride in the king's carriage and shun the poor man's cart. They write history as if the little man did not exist except as background for aristocracy.

:-:

Somehow our historians have lost their feeling for human justice and plain humanity when a successful marauder is called a great military leader instead of what he should be called—a killer at large.

It is astonishing to see a nation as great as France allot a temple in the heart of the city of Paris to a bloodthirsty, self-seeking tyrant like Napoleon, and bedeck it with flags and cockades of freedom on people's holidays—but such is historic forgetfulness, and such is historic confusion, when good men are buried in the sand and the evil in a marble casket.

Historic Figures

The reader of today meets the old historic figures all planed out and polished up; they appeared quite different to their contemporaries before all the roughness and unevenness was smoothed out by history.

History

Half the world is still engaged in the ancient struggle for freedom from the shackles put on by usurping ideologues. The wrathful gods of old stepped aside for Karl Marx, but the Red princelings differ little from the celestial ones in applying scorpions and the lash to the lowly.

:-:

Frequently in history the burden rested on men behind the screen; the fancy and proud actors on the stage were only marionettes.

:-:

History of our global events is merely an insignificant whisper on the fringe of the titanic battles of the cosmos, our blood-and tear-soaked earth but a splinter falling in the aeonic conflicts.

:-:

History repeats its mistakes but not its accomplishments.

:-:

Of the lives of the oppressors in history there should be only one brief note identifying their tenebrous existence; the rest of it, with castle, equestrian statue, fancy dress with crown and mace and bloody sword, ought to go into a black book filled with horror tales and pitiful songs. Social understanding lies in searching for the life and work and suffering of the little people whose memory seems all but buried beneath the showy tinsel of the people's malefactors.

:-:

There are too few books from the pen of those who made history and too many by those who poorly retraced it.

:-:

Every historian writes as if his little country were the center of the globe—and nothing can convince him otherwise.

:-:

History should be taught backwards. It makes for a more somber panorama. We did not climb from rags to riches. We still fight for waterways and island rights like growling cavemen, we grovel before arrogant overlords and sneer and hiss at men of other color.

:-:

History is a planless sequence of little events and situations. Had England remained a peninsula, as it was not so long ago, Napoleon might have conquered all of Europe and the British Empire perhaps would never have come to be.

If the Czar had executed Lenin instead of imprisoning him, Russia likely would have stayed a liberal socialist country under Kerenski.

If the Babylonian Jews had come to the rescue of beleaguered Jerusalem in the year 70 instead of defaulting on their promise of assistance, Judea would perhaps have lived on.

:-:

A thousand little things—a poorly directed dagger or bullet, a geographical oddity, a quirk of circumstance—and the world would have taken a different shape.

:-:

History has three sides to it: the wrong side, the right side, and the way it really happened.

:-:

Glory is the most precious gift posterity can bestow upon its deserving ancestors. It is one measure which even the most powerful of potentates can neither falsify nor escape. If there is any glory to the Imperium Romanum, it lies in the ruins of the temples which they destroyed, not in the gory epics of their conquests and victories. I do not wish to know the ugly details of how the mercenary legions vanquished neighbor after neighbor. I do not want to know the sinister data of their evil hierarchy that began with Romulus and ran its sanguinary course through the Western world for a thousand years and more. I say it matters little what Caesar befouled his own mother and what Messalina put womanhood to shame. Furthermore, I would say that all that type of history is not a history of the people, but rather of its exploiters, its usurpers, its false prophets.

The wars of conquest by self-appointed or family-perpetuated masters over an enslaved people are not the history of the world, but rather the story of man's iniquity and unspeakable cruelty to fellow man. The hardships and tortures with which usurpers and their like terrorized mankind are a terrible, but only a single, chapter in the great book of the story of man, to be read like the verse on Purgatory as a reminder and a lesson. The story of man begins where the chapter of tyranny ends and he who embellishes the misdeeds of the blackguards, be they ancient or of recent vintage, teaches not history but the perversion of it.

Come forth, the man to tell the story of the little people, people that till the earth and raise the fruit, that fish in the ocean and lakes and rivers and hunt in the forests and breed the stock and trade in the markets and make a thousand things of use or of pleasure for man and child. Come forth, the man to tell the story of these people, the real people, those that work and those that pray, those that wander and sing and play and lead the good life and have fellowship in their hearts and sincerity in their hands.

These are the people who deserve the glory that posterity can bestow. Their world should be written about. How they fared and how they failed should be related in the books of history, and not, certainly not, all that plush and plunder, that weird twosome of tournament and dungeon that signifies the era of courtly tyranny blighting mankind like the plague it was.

:-:

There are as many versions of history as there are nations, and then some.

:-:

History has named so many ugly despots wise, so many wrong ones just and so many puny ones great, that the unbiased student of the past exclaims "Scoundrel!" whenever he faces laurel on a statue.

:-:

What lessons can the young learn from history if the most poisonous and perfidious despots are daily honored by a superstitious and forgetful people?

:-:

It is time to cleanse our books and songs, our homes and schools, our streets and churches, even our very cemeteries, of the symbols glorifying savage princes of the past and relegate their horrid images to the somber pages of criminal history.

:-:

To study history without considering its

ethical implication is like studying law without an understanding of right and wrong.

A crime is not less meaningful because it occurred generations ago, and evil is no less pronounced because distant nations or remote ancestors suffered its effect; tyranny shall not be pampered because it succeeded nor shall goodness and nobility be trifled with because they failed.

:-:

We have to examine history, just as we do current happenings, for the purposes of the original source of information, and apply to it the same value judgments as we do news of the hour.

:-:

It is time to show the true face of history—the history of the people and not that of their exploiters, the history of free people who were made into slaves, the history of peaceable people who were vanquished—and to show in this true light the persons of reckless ambition and malevolence who made the world we live in a jungle of mutual destruction for the glory and vanity and ugly avarice of the very few, their henchmen and their sycophants.

174 |

From days so far back that for a record of them we have to dig for documents deep in the sands and at the bottom of the seas, to the very hour we live in, the evidence of evil can be heard and seen and it is no less horrible to behold today than it was in the past. Indeed, no outrage committed by the tyrants of old can outdo those perpetrated before our very eyes in this very generation.

More people have been put to death—men, women and children—in the most grotesque manner by Hitler, Stalin and Mao during the lifetime of the reader of this book than have been slaughtered in all written history. Perhaps, if we clearly and solemnly look at the past, our vision of the present will be more concise.

:-:

It is time to make an end to the macabre farce that calls itself history, but is no more than an enumeration of acts of violence and expropriation committed by princely greed and avarice. Let these deeds be dealt with as what they are: acts of criminality; and let such criminality be told as little as is necessary, in admonition of new generations to uphold justice and disavow tyranny. Let history be dedicated to describing clearly and unmistakably the misery that has befallen mankind for ten thousand years, during which it has been held in bondage and misused by cunning usurpers. Let history dwell at length, not on the data connected with princely criminals, but on the tragically few light moments when noble men held the leadership and their fellow citizens lived in dignity and freedom.

:-:

A man becomes an historic figure when the world has forgotten all the little things about him and remembers just one big one.

:-:

We must judge historic events, not by what leaders did for themselves, but rather by what they did for humanity.

Hobby
Is a man's endeavor to make an avocation give him satisfaction an occupation should.

Holy Men
All these holy freaks of India, those who stick needles through their cheeks, who lie down on a bed of nails, who scorch themselves with fire and thorn—there is not an ounce of true faith in this army of beggars, as there never

was among the flagellants or thistle-eaters of
Europe. These men are common exhibitionists
living a panhandler's life, half-witted and half-
believing. It only shows how far people will go
to escape working.

Home
The home one runs away from is none.

:-:

Home is where your friends are.

Homiletics
I wish they would remember that Moses was
a poor speaker; still his was the voice of God.

Honesty
Toward oneself is rare indeed.

:-:

The confidence man has honesty always on
his lips.

Honor
Is so frequently bestowed upon the wrong,
the false and the scheming that it has become a
prize rather than a virtue.

:-:

Honor and dignity are matters of cognition, not recognition.

:-:

One should be honored only for what one does for others, not for what one does for himself. Honoring a person for personal accomplishments is like paying him for doing some good. Honor the helpful, not the self-centered. Throw not bouquets at the feet of the prima donna, or the victor at the boxing match, or the skilled peacock financier; rather throw the bouquet at the feet of those silent and selfless workers in behalf of the poor, the downtrodden, the ailing and the aged.

The kings who invited the gifted to their palace honored not the artists but rather themselves. They draped the poets, the painters, the playwrights around their court like so much decorative bunting.

Hope
Is the attractive escape-hatch from the harsh alternative to do or die into a world of tranquilizing daydreams.

:-:

Fear is the mother of hope.

:-:

Whatever betterment we have today was carved out of a world of stone by men of the hammer, not men of hope.

:-:

Hope may ease the troubled conscience but not the trouble itself.

:-:

Where faith takes no decisive action, decision is left to fate.

Hospitality
Remember, the man with whom you converse is a guest at your mind.

Hostility
Begins at home. If school does not eradicate it, life has little chance.

Humane Associations
There are a number of Humane Associations in Alabama, Mississippi and Georgia. But their concern is with the welfare of animals, not humans. In fact, only recently they offered a substantial prize for a painless mousetrap. Perhaps some day their sentiments will evolve from mice, rats and rabbits to their black neighbors across the aisle.

Humanities

Without the humanities science is merely a conglomerate of deadly cold facts; and without God the humanities are merely an assemblage of arid cultural information.

It is God or the recognition of an everlasting ethical principle, that can give education a face, and give this face the view of a better tomorrow.

Humanness

The scope of humane courses differs from century to century; the underlying motivation, however, is always the same.

Humbleness

Before a principle is the meaning of a man's faith and character.

Humility

It takes a lot of thought to fathom human knowledge, and rare intellectual humility to realize that the greatest depth of man's thinking still runs only in shallow grooves.

Humor

Is a gracious arbiter.

:-:

Humor is the harbinger of persuasion; lack of it foretells discord.

:-:

A sense of humor is sense for sure.

:-:

Humor is the daughter of reason; she makes game of self-important pretentiousness.

Hunger
Hunger is the father of servility.

Hypocrisy
Where terror reigns, hypocrisy will raise its changing faces.

I

I and They

The greatest of struggles are within you, not without; in nations, too, the most crucial battles were fought not against an outside enemy.

Iconoclasm

I am waiting for the day of iconoclasm when the devil's horsemen will be pulled into the gutter, when the fratricidal kings and the crimson-fingered queens, from Isabella of the Inquisition to the lecherous nymphomaniac Catherine, will have their portraits thrown into the cellars of museums, and our edifices, streets and forests are named after the men who fought for freedom and justice instead of the slavers and their henchmen.

Idea

The world may be only an idea of mine, but my idea is not this kind of world.

Idealism

Idealism is an approach to life, not an end to itself. One can be quite materialistic about so-called ideal things, such as religion, literature and the arts. On the other hand, one can be quite idealistic about material things, such as the living conditions of the working or farming man.

:-:

It is the cause that makes for idealism, not the devotion to it. Even the Devil himself commands devotees.

Ideas

Words, profound and meaningless, pop out when thought fails.

:-:

More people have died for false idols than true ideas.

Identity

Basically, all people are alike. That is perhaps the cause of their constant squabbles and feuds; they dislike in each other their own debilities.

Idleness

Don't kill time—you may yet discover you could have used it.

:-:

Idlenesss is preoccupation with the barnacles of thought.

Idolatry

Idolize ideas, not men. The God of the Hebrews prohibited the making of His image. He wanted no idolators, but believers.

Idols

If it be true that one becomes like what he worships, what monsters this world's idols must be!

Ignorance

It is not the ignorant who forever keep the Devil's brew boiling, but rather the cunning and their erudite friends.

:-:

Most people don't care enough to search for the facts of the issues they talk about with such concern.

Illusion

If this be all just an illusion, take away the world and leave me my dreams!

Image

It is tragic that in their declining years so many neglect to protect their original image in the eyes of the world they shall leave behind. So many destroy their image by years of senility or obstinacy.

While many men die too early, others die too late.

Imagination

Reality—what a poor substitute for imagination!

:-:

Imagination is the arena of the genius.

:-:

Science, too, must ride Pegasus—diligence its legs, but imagination its wings.

:-:

Heaven is a matter of imagination but so are hate, love, and pretty much everything else.

Imitation

Is nine-tenths of our cultural pattern.

Immaculate Birth

Christianity is only one of the many religions and sects that accept virgin or fleshless birth. Many Hindu swamis, such as Vivekananda, proclaimed themselves *avatar,* God born into flesh of a virgin mother. But none of the Hindu semigods insisted on acceptance of such claims.

Immorality

Acts of animalism are nothing more than that; immoral they are not. Immorality occurs only when there exists an antagonistic tendency or act against society.

:-:

No act is immoral by which the perpetrator harms no one except himself or herself.

In a world so full of evil suppressive laws and measures, it is quite unimportant what men and also women do with their bodies, in the intimacy of their homes, and nothing changes the character or the harmlessness of those engagements if gifts are part of the game.

It matters little to the good Lord if some Hungarian actress or a Hollywood starlet accepts a bracelet or a mink coat as a souvenir for a weekend, or if a poor girl in Marseilles receives a ten-franc note for similar accommodations. We publicize in Paris, in London, in New York, the foreplay of high-toned Hollywood prostitutes. Why then denigrate, even incarcerate, a simple young female whose erotic enterprises are on a more primitive scale?

Immortality

Is no more fabulous than birth: that out of dust and dirt can rise an organism of a billion muscles, nerves and bones, to talk and walk and think and then dry up and bury itself back into a hole of dirt and dust. Who can fathom the whereto and wherefore of life immortal?

:-:

In passing away we only take to the heavens what we leave to mankind.

:-:

The truly great from Lao-tse to Spinoza never discussed life after death, only before it.

:-:

Some behave as if they would jump out of life into eternity with all their jewelry, medals and furs. Immortality is not there, but here. Immortality is not what you find there, but what you leave behind.

:-:

Of course there is immortality; I just hate clerics describing it as if they had just returned from it.

Immutability
Great men die but great ideas live on.

Incompetence
We now live in the Era of Incompetence; we have painters who can't paint, poets who can't rhyme and composers who whistle dissonance.

Independence
Is the wish of a peasant: to raise porridge with his own two hands.

The free man wants to live, create and work in interdependence. Man is to man a Devil but sometimes a God.

Index
The trouble with the Index of the Catholic Church is that it prohibits works attacking God; it should rather forbid books that attack man.

188 |

Spinoza's *Ethics* are on the Index, but Hitler's *Mein Kampf* is not.

Indifference

Being wrong is no disgrace, being indifferent is.

:-:

There is no greater temptation than that of indifference.

Indolence

Takes others for granted, but graver yet is the consequence of taking oneself for granted.

Infidel

Is one who does not accept the superstitions of his community.

Influence

There comes a time when the twig can no longer be bent.

Inhibitions

If we could *see* desires, if greeds and lusts, hates and envies, jealousies and revulsions, the whole array of human feelings had a corporeal form, this would be an impossible world; it is the sobering social inhibitions that make co-existence tolerable.

:-:

It isn't the lack of inhibitions that distinguishes man from man but rather the choice of inhibitions. The lack of inhibitions merely distinguishes animal from man.

Inhumanity

There are many examples of present-day man's inhumanity to man. Their great number prohibits enumeration. But the sordid deeds are known to all. Be it that opposing gangsters are assassinated in front of television sets in Cuba with the entire city population of Havana cheering every detail of the butchery; be it that an oil-guided satyr of Araby sits on the throne of a realm where every fifth person is a bound slave, kidnaped from the plains of Africa and sold in the market place—for the favor of such dastardly creatures these things are viewed by the leaders of the West with a benevolent smile and by those of the East with brotherly embrace.

:-:

With all the bestiality ghosting around this world, why should anyone fear God? Could God in his most intense wrath do worse than Hitler?

No hell or predatory deity can outdo man's inhumanity to man.

Inquisition

Popes conspired with kings and knaves against Anti-Popes and against the lowly people, and Anti-Popes conspired with upstarts and adventurers against all standards of decency and humanity. Popes initiated the most cruel forms of inquisitorial torture to rob the Jews, Moslems and others professing alleged deviations from the true faith, in order to deprive these unfortunate persons of their properties and privileges. In time such inquisition corporations became the wealthiest organizations in medieval Europe, and in more modern centuries one heard repeated complaints from Catholic inquisitors that there were hardly any more worthwhile objects to be examined; there were only poor fish left in the shallow waters of the See.

Insanity

It has become downright modish to claim a touch of madness. Some women speak of their psychiatrist as of their hairdresser or modiste—a sort of confessor-in-waiting.

:-:

Insanity is a frequent visitor of genius under stress, a strange guest of the lonely in their flight from reality.

:-:

The insane mind has as many variations as the sane; sometimes I wonder which one contributes more to the madness of the world.

:-:

Of the very same actions and expressions some were declared to be suffering from religious mania, others were called saints and divines.

:-:

Perhaps not all confined in asylums are insane, but quite a few on the loose, are.

Instructions

Teach kindness and you reap intelligence; teach hate and you reap prejudice.

Integrity

They teach you early how to wash your face and body, in school and home, but how to cleanse your mind of putrid ideas and prejudice, that is left unsaid and thus undone. I am afraid that even the occasional ablutions in the church are scarcely purifying, no more than face-saving. They walk about with shining faces and soiled souls.

Intemperance

Is an annoyance, but controlled enmity is something to look out for.

Interesting

Even the dullest is interesting when speaking his mind honestly; it is the scintillating surface conversationalist who is the intolerable bore.

Intimacy

Living together in close quarters doesn't necessarily make for intimacy.

Intuition

Is thinking ahead, as reason is thinking back.

Issues

Handle people with gloves; but issues, bare-fisted.

J

Jails

Stables designed to improve ethics by herding together the sinners. As sin will always come out on top, the result of this process is invariably the acquisition of at least one new sin by the old sinners.

:-:

You cannot make a man straight by cuffing him to crooks.

:-:

It is quite often the wrong people who are in the jails, while those who belong in them are sitting high up in society, not only in this country, but even more so in other lands.

:-:

The great torturers of Stalin and Hitler are at large, while little people fill the jails. Truly here, the guilty were not those in the docks but rather those on the judge's bench.

Jest

Is but honeyed criticism.

Jesters

Are of two different brands: those with wit and those with venom.

Jesus

The best we can say, is that of the life of Jesus we truly know only that He died.

:-:

When you weep for Jesus, weep more yet for His brothers because their suffering was greater, and the strength that was His was not in them. While He was buried by His people, His brethren were devoured by beasts of prey.

Jew

What blasphemy is the theology of crucifixion—to paint the Jew as the destroyer of religion when the Jew is really its creator.

:-:

Jews have been stunted in their growth by a hostile world from the days of Israel, the God fighter. They were chosen by the Lord to carry the Tablets of the Law, but their neighbors wanted them to carry the cross, or the banner of the crescent.

The chosen ones were decimated, decade after decade, century after century, with forced conversion, rack and pyre and noxious gases, and what could have been by now a nation of a hundred million children of Israel, is left a poor people after two millennia without grace and charity.

:-:

Many attribute to the Jews their own failing and then hate them for it.

:-:

Jews are the heart-people of our era. Could you see Jesus as a German, Frenchman or Chinese? Or Paul as a Japanese or Scotsman?

:-:

Everybody meets the kind of Jew he expects.

:-:

John Adams wrote in a letter to Van der Kamp that "he ordained the Jews to be the most essential instrument for civilizing the nations." Well, they failed.

:-:

Whom did they hate before the Jews became a people?

:-:

Less than one-half of one percent of the world's population is of Hebrew origin. Still, almost one-third of all Nobel Prize winners are Jews; almost one-third of the great physicists, mathematicians, medical discoverers and musical performers are Jews.

What a handicap God's gift can be.

Jew Abhorrers

Every year a new generation of Jew abhorrers is called into life by the teaching of the sordid theology of crucifixion. Relentlessly, with sanctimonious demeanor, the ministers of loving Jesus impress the naive little ones with the story of Golgotha, the brutal slaying of God at the behest of Jews.

And from then on the innocent hearts of the children at the services or Sunday schools become a wounded receptacle of the subtle poison of fear and horror, turning the churches of gentle Jesus into temples of hate.

Jew Hatred

They want us to forgive the killing of six

million Jews while they can't forgive us the supposed killing of one.

:-:

You can't be a Christian and an anti-Semite; Jesus was a Semite before he declared himself Christ.

Jewish Sin

Nazism and Christianity have this in common: they both make the Jew responsible for all evil in the world; and both Nazism and Christianity mark the Jew a congenital offender by his very existence.

The anti-Jewish preachings of Christianity were and still are the seedbed from which Hitlerism flowers.

The Catholicism of John XXIII, a rare Pope indeed, admits its Jew-baiting references in prayer and other rituals were gratuitous and could be omitted, just as the charge of deicide against the Hebrew nation was false theology as Jesus *wanted* to die to redeem mankind. This is a rather belated effort at the grave of many million Jews, defamed, mutilated and massacred for so many centuries.

It was all a horrible mistake, a stunned Catholic clergy admits ecumenically; the death of Christ was a providentially desired sacrifice for the sake of all sinful mankind and not a political killing by Jews.

But if the Jewish nation of today and all times before bears no guilt, that implies that the Church was false in libeling the Jews throughout its history.

Journalism
Is characterized no less by its topics than by their treatment.

Judaism
Has no sects, only attitudes. What does it matter where one meets God and His Beatitude, be it in one great principle or in numerous precepts and legends?

:-:

Judaism is the story of a great father popularized by two difficult offspring.

:-:

Christianity is a faith tied to a man; Judaism is a faith tied to God.

Judgment
Listening to both sides does not necessarily bring about a correct judgment.

:-:

To those who sit in judgment:

Every man has at least once in his lifetime prepared an act that is or has been in one or another of the historic civilizations considered a capital crime: from eating forbidden food, stealing a loaf of bread or addressing a taboo person to praising a disgraced person or deity or wearing a wrong medal.

Judgment Day

If only the Earth could heave off her coat of green and show the billion wounds of her inter-red children which men have inflicted.

:-:

To resurrect the nations underground would be as futile as making the living stay on forever. Let tomorrow's youth be raised on deeds of kindness, and the rest forgotten.

Justice

Is the handmaiden of government and thus bespeaks the character of its master: the vilest tortures have as often been declared law as well as the loftiest precepts.

:-:

In certain countries, judges seem to act according to predicament, not precedent.

:-:

Justice is more a question of attitude than fact.

:-:

Stand on the side of the weaker and you'll always be on the right side.

:-:

Justice is a poor substitute for compassion.

:-:

Justice is like a greased pig: many touch it, few hold on to it.

:-:

I do not plead for the abolition of the law, but rather for the investiture of justice.

:-:

Run not to the Lord with your little complaints; you might distract his attention from the great evil that hovers over this globe.

:-:

Kant postulated immortality to prove justice possible in the hereafter. If Providence is unjust here, I am afraid it is no better after.

Juveniles
Will drift into delinquency if there are no

chores to do, no tasks cut out. America has eliminated the apprentice shop for the non-studious. The towns are full of idle juveniles who are kept *per forma* in school but *realiter* in the gutter. The truant at thirteen might better be an apprentice at fourteen than a delinquent schoolboy.

K

Keenness

It takes a rough stone to sharpen the edge.

Kera

They all have it. *Kera.* The Cabbalists refer to it as one eye on the realms of glittering everyday values. Few are the starry-eyed with only one Lord, one aim and one love.

Killing

Not to kill is a noble request, but if the fighters for freedom had not killed, they would still be wearing leg irons.

Kinship

A man after my own heart means a man with my own prejudices.

Klan

Jesus never stopped in Georgia but Lucifer did.

Knights

There are those who carry a lion on their shield and a hyena in their heart.

Knowledge

It takes a lot of knowledge to understand how little we know.

:-:

Learn what you know and not what is alien. Can the worm in the stomach see the light of the moon?

We think in the light of our planetary group of rocks, which we euphemistically call "the universe." This is as little the universe as man's stomach, although the latter may appear as the world of worlds to a worm or germ.

All conjectures beyond our firmaments of space and thought are theological dream-spinning and no more, fantasies of one fungus on a speck of dust talking to another on the nature of powers beyond.

:-:

There is no knowledge—only a lesser state of ignorance.

:-:

Knowledge *may* be good; kindness is good.

:-:

Knowledge dwells in three mansions: the house of words, the home of facts, and the niche of wisdom. It is the last only that harbors peace of mind.

:-:

Only the ignorant know everything.

:-:

Some are satisfied when they hear it, some when they see it, and others when they have a Greek word for it; only too few go beyond the word.

:-:

The paramount issue is not to know more but to do better.

:-:

He was so steeped in knowledge that not once did he trouble to look up and face life.

:-:

It seems that much of what we know is not worth beholding and quite a lot that is worthy we do not know.

:-:

It is easier to acquire knowledge than to use it.

K Z

When you see the enslaved in a concentration camp turning on friend and kin in desperate efforts of self-preservation, judge not the derelict victims but their savage tormentors.

L

Labor

The many live for it so the few may live off it.

:-:

The laborer is not a better man than the capitalist, only less fortunate.

Language

You may use the same words and still speak a different language.

:-:

The Yugoslavs understand Russian and the Russians understand Yugoslav, but neither understands the other.

:-:

Language makes not the man; it is the man who makes language. Perhaps our schools would do better to guide the young in a search for the truer thought, the deeper concept, instead of a better syntax.

Last Words

May your last words be like your first: a cry for the nearness of loved ones.

Law

Is as varied as the sentiments of those who rule.

:-:

A law is as proper as the motives of the ruler.

:-:

A law is never holy but often sinful. And perhaps even today, in this freest of countries of all times and places, there may be many who stand on the wrong side of the law, placed thus not because they went astray, but rather because the law strayed from the right path.

It is the lawbreakers in our history who have brought to the people of the Western world the rights they enjoy, and if the enchained East is to come to its freedom, it will again be the lawbreakers who will tumble the overbearing colossus of legitimate totalitarianism.

:-:

The law is the crime it purports to prevent.

It is with the breaking of the law that the freedom of man began; the bills of rights were written with the blood of heretics and law-breakers.

:-:

Only those who punish lovingly punish justly.

:-:

Law is naked force in the cloak of justice, from Pharaoh to the latest party chairman.

:-:

Many of our eminent philosophers of law, like Aristotle, Hobbes, Hegel, were so involved in the forest of legalism that they never could pay attention to the modest tree of man.

There were, however, unforgettable and never-to-be-forgotten exceptions, such as More, Spinoza, Rousseau, Lessing, Tolstoy.

:-:

Law, unfortunately, relies so much upon concealment and so little upon understanding.

:-:

The word "law" or "legality" in no way implies justice, fairness or equity. Indeed, some of the most cruel, tyrannical precepts were and are masqueraded under the name "law." Hitler's Nuremberg Law, the feudal *jus primae noctis* that gave the lord of the manor the privilege of the first night with any and every bride in his realm, the Slave Acts of our Southern states, the laws of bondage that predominated as late as the eighteenth century, the laws of servitude of the serfs and villeins—all these monstrous aggressive regulations paraded through history under the presumptive title of laws.

The law is nothing but the statutory and often willful operation of the desires and often malevolent intents of a ruling community or a ruling individual. The cadis in the Middle East have, with sanctimonious indifference, ordered unbelievable mutilations of the poor, starving devil who would steal a chicken from the market place. And with equal indifference, the Communist People's Court will execute a hungry comrade for appropriating a bag of flour.

At the time of Benjamin Franklin's funeral, a twelve-year-old girl was lawfully executed by hanging, in the town of London, for stealing her mistress's winter coat.

It would be easy to assemble from only known history a thousand-page volume listing the bestialities perpetrated upon man in the name of one law or another.

The law is not a holy cow. It is more like a rabid jackal.

:-:

The law is not a symbol of justice, but rather an expression of the wishes and desires of those in dominance, and only in parts of the Western democracies have laws even a semblance of fair dealing and fair play.

:-:

It is noteworthy that totalitarian despots who have succeeded in reducing the state to their private domain excel in upholding its sanctity and inviolability.

:-:

In our own generation, in the lifetime of most readers of this page, the law of Nazi Germany apprehended in less than a decade six million men, women and children of the Jewish faith, dragged them from all four corners of Europe into starvation camps and then put them to death in such cruel manner as would stagger the mind of a common criminal.

All this was done by a lawfully elected government under the authority given to it by the law of the land and with the approval of thousands of eminent judges and other functionaries of the German law who wrote the code for the apprehension and execution of native and foreign-born Jews living in Europe at that time. And, as has been observed, most of these jurists who made, passed and approved the Nazi laws are either still in high office or drawing retirement pensions from their grateful government because the law is the law and these jurists are entitled by law to their jobs or pensions.

:-:

The abuse of the black man in our own Southern states is by no means as provocative as that in the Republic of South Africa, but here as well as there it is the law which is the offender and it is justice that is offended. The degradation and humiliation of a citizen is an evil in itself, and no sound discussion of law or justice is possible unless we accept this premise.

:-:

It is needless to enumerate cases of judicial inconsistency. Every intelligent observer could relate from his own experience cases of trifles being turned into crimes by law, and criminals trifling with our law because of its vagaries.

:-:

Governors have perjured themselves to bring false testimony against citizens of darker hue to keep them out of their schools, voting places and business offices, and so have the legislators,

212 |

the judges and the clerks. Too many freedom-fighting students are in jail as lawbreakers, while Governors Wallace and Faubus are still the arbiters of legality in the South.

:-:

The law—so swift in its arrest of a dowdy scrubwoman who sneaks a pair of stockings into her shopping bag!—this same law sees no murder when an arrogant demagogue belches out his obscene demands to stone the "niggers."

:-:

There isn't a man or woman alive who hasn't, at one time or another, done something for which he or she could be punished severely indeed because of a breach of the law.

Why, then, should those who have failed because of either weakness or ignorance or economic pressure or mental aberration or emotional distress or involvement through friends or family, why should those who are only weak be dealt with like beasts in a stockyard?

:-:

Those who are incorrigibly malevolent and violent need to be eliminated from our society, but as to the rest, they need to be advised and rehabilitated, not punished.

:-:

I fail to see the relationship between one hundred destroyed parking tickets and seven years living in a criminal zoo. I fail to see the relationship betwen a man involved in a homosexual entanglement with another man and five years in a criminal zoo. I fail to see the relationship between a man trying to hide some of his earnings from the government's collection agency and ten years in a criminal zoo. I fail to see the relationship between a man selling homemade liquor and eight years in a criminal zoo. I fail to see the relationship between a weak man sniffing poisonous drugs and three years in a criminal zoo. I fail to see the relationshp between a mixed-up girl or an unstable woman getting cash instead of a bracelet for giving her pleasures and one year in a criminal zoo—I could go on and on.

:-:

Perhaps a new concept, a new term should evolve that would enable a more enlightened judiciary to make a clear distinction between recidivist, malevolent, hardened, antisocial criminals and those many who do what is prohibited, not because they are enemies of society, but rather because they are somehow victims of themselves. The human who does away with a newborn fetus because it came to life without arms and feet is not to be judged by the same panel and by the same paragraph as the mugger in the dark street killing a passer-by. Indeed, those persons whose failings and offenses originate deep in their mental, emotional or hereditary inadequacy should be judged not by officials of the court and not by their peers, but rather by their patrons. An organization of patrons is essential to deal with those who fail society not out of vice or viciousness, but out of weakness of body and soul. They need help, not punishment; they need guidance, not incarceration; they need assistance, not castigation, they need rehabilitation, not retention; they are victims, not violators.

:-:

Justice is based on understanding, and not on tradition. Law by precedent can be a travesty of justice. Judging by precedent, we would still have to hang "witches" on the basis of mere denunciation and bury them with a stake through their hearts. Judging by precedent, we would have to hang every thief regardless of circumstances. Judging by precedent, we would have to shoot every deserter and mutilate every gossip and jail every debtor who couldn't pay his rent.

Law by precedent is a lingering shadow of feudalistic darkness and medieval superstition.

:-:

Open the doors of the slave compounds and let go all of those who are not vicious and violent. Then look within your own community and apprehend those law-erudite tricksters of jurisprudence who incite people to hate, to deeds of violence, to acts of perfidy, suppression and disparagement. Apprehend the Wallaces, the Rockwells, the Barnetts. Apprehend those who despoil the dignity and the freedom of this or any other land, and let them take the place —if you wish to fill your prisons—of the confused and displaced poor who somehow did not master the working of their humble economy.

Put the assassins, the demagogues, the lynchers and the rioters into the coldness of those cells and show the poor who have failed the road back to restitution by rehabilitation. Let there be justice in the courts instead of law.

:-:

The man in China has no right of assembly, no freedom of press or speech, no right to strike or travel, no right to conjugal living with his family, no rights to any property no matter how small, no choice of work or leisure—in fact, he is just a nameless cog in the machinery of the commune. Still the law of China as set down in its Red constitution reads like a parchment of people's privileges. Jurists made it read like that at the behest of Mao, who masterminded the code.

The King of Arabia, whose personal executioner chops off a citizen's hand because he stole an orange, feels no regrets or compunctions because the monarch appears convinced he is only carrying out the letter of the law. Neither does the King of Saudi Arabia suffer remorse in taxing the sale in the open market of slave girls to be debauched by sheiks and sundry. Such is the law.

And the heads of the Western, as well as the so-called Socialist world, vie for the favors of these two and other law-observing Kings.

In our own Southern states we have a law with two sets of books, one for whites only and one for whites in their relationship with blacks. The second set of law books, however, is based purely on precedent: the punishments of the blacks are inscribed in bloody red; punishment

for whites who sin against the Negroes is written in disappearing ink.

:-:

The law is a book of prison rules within
which the common people live. It was written
by learned men at the pleasure of the masters
and always reads as if God-given and morally
ordained. There never was a shortage of scholars to do the bidding of the exalted. There
never was a precept too mean, be it in Dixie or
Stalin-land, failing to receive a sanctimonious
and scholarly rationalization.

:-:

The law needs to be taken out of the hands
of the offenders and given to the people who
will administer it not as a code for the power-
greedy and power-drunk, but for the welfare of
the common man.

:-:

In the state of Vermont, the highest penalty
for rape is a fine of $2,000—the fine for a theft
of $2,000 is 5 to 10 years in bondage. What a
low price to pay for terror and inhumanity,
what a fearful price to pay for property!

:-:

In the state of Indiana, there died recently Henry Sullivan, aged 85, who served 63 years of imprisonment because at the age of 14 he stole twenty dollars' worth of machinery from an abandoned mill.

:-:

In one of our Southern states white neighbors of a grown woman beat to death a fourteen-year-old black boy for whistling at her. Known to the local and federal authorities, they could not be punished. Such is the double-standard law in that state.

:-:

The law dwells on property offenses. It is a throwback to feudal days—or perhaps it never entirely emerged from them. All crimes are understandable except those against Crown property. You can beat a Negro boy to death for whistling at a white girl, and the law will look the other way, but let the man steal a bag of corn and he is in for it. You can kill four black people, as they did in Macon, Georgia, in 1946, and the law never saw it; but steal a car in Georgia and you will be on the chain gang for more years than the week has days. Drive a black girl out of a school with blows and four-letter words, and the law will see no evil; but run off with a ten-dollar bill from the counter, and the law will get you. In the good old days of the Wild West you could beat a man one-eyed, and the town would laugh; but steal a horse, and they would hang you.

The law puts no value on man's dignity, and little on his security, but an awful lot on his property.

:-:

The kings are gone, the nobles are gone, but their law is still with us. It is time to break the law of the past, and let us have the law of tomorrow—not with regard to property and position, but with regard to dignity and liberty, and the true independence of all citizens, and let those who fall under the pressure of economic strains be dealt with in a helpful manner toward rehabilitation, instead of being reduced to caged animals.

Laymen
We are all laymen, only some more so than others.

Learning
It is the learned who forever threaten the peace of man—not the illiterates, but the Ramses, the Attilas, Caesars, Mao, Mussolini. What

ever they and their entourages lacked, it was not learning.

:-:

Learning of the brain will further the ability to create new appliances for human comfort— but what of human peace?

:-:

Speak to your own self and let it teach you.

:-:

Honor is a poor reward for the pleasures of study. Where honor is set as the price of education, the mind may pack in many facts and data in its hasty reach for the goal, but the heart will become forbidding and corrupted.

:-:

Education must serve a purpose or it may fall into "decay." Tradition had a grip on the school as a parcel of princely property, and to use such property on behalf of the Crown was the scope of tradition. Such scope is unchanged in the lands which are vassals to totalitarian masters, where the youth is no more than a chunk of state property manipulated, like all of life, limb and holdings, for the benefit of a demagogic clique. But in the free lands, youth is not a means but a goal, each person to be respected as a body and mind in his own right, to be dealt with not in competition and tasteless comparison.

In our free society we aim to treat the porter with the same regard as the pundit, the janitor like the judge, the pauper like the millionaire. Upon such equality our social organization is based, and in such equality our youth is to be raised. The poor in memory, the poor in perception, the slow in thinking and the weak in diligence are to be handled with the very same gentility as those enriched in all respects.

A child can as little help being lesser mentally as it can help being so physically. There is as little fairness in catering to the gifted and setting back the deprived as there is in constantly praising the beauties of a pretty child and noting the defects, scars and pimples of a homely one.

Leisure

People go to great lengths to get their working time reduced; then they take this hard-won time—and kill it.

:-:

Leisure is the dream-time of doing nothing spun by the many who stay on the wrong job.

:-:

The great hunt of the masses: to kill time.

Lie

Some would search and twist to come to truth, while others do the same to protect a lie.

:-:

To come face to face with the truth of today, we must bare the lies of yesterday.

Life

Is a rather short walk through eternity. Be they seeds, pups or infants, on the trek all pick up weight, sensitivity and awareness. Then, much before the end of the run, they deteriorate, head, legs and lungs. The tragicomedy of existence: the long walk of slow decay.

:-:

It is not how old you are that matters, but how many hours of your life you have yet to live.

:-:

Man creative lives many lives; some men are so dull they do not live even once.

:-:

Life is so crowded with everyday, it takes

great effort to step aside and just watch and think.

:-:

Few only live their own life; so many have it lived by others.

:-:

Many are so preoccupied preparing themselves for life that when they are about ready, it has already passed them by.

Life Hereafter

They sacrifice a lamb to Baal so their cattle may double and treble. They sacrifice a calf so their trade may prosper, they sacrifice a virgin so they may win a war—and the good little people with the little faith, they sacrifice comfort and cash so they may buy a life hereafter.

I do not deny the life hereafter, but I do not think it is for sale.

:-:

So many who know little or nothing of this world speak with amazing certainty of the next one.

Life Span

It is less important to extend life in length than in depth.

Listening

Many words remain unspoken when men are deeply moved and only those who listen with the inner ear can hear them.

:-:

The most precious thing a man can lend is his ears.

Literacy

Has not abolished the world's grievous problems, wars and tyranny, but it has made a greater number of victims of them.

:-:

Literacy is rather a new thing. A mere two hundred years ago even in such countries as Russia, Austria, France and Italy, only one out of ten could read and write. In many nations of Asia and Africa similar conditions still prevail.

:-:

But one thing we realized after these two hundred years: it is as easy to misunderstand the written word as the spoken word. The greatest crimes of our century were perpetrated not by still illiterate people such as Bedouins, Libyans or Tibetans, but rather by the most book-learned, the Germans.

:-:

A billion people more can read now than could fifty years ago. Unfortunately, especially in the East, this means a billion more of the gullible whom the wrong persons can reach not only by the spoken but also by the printed word.

Literati

Taking a pose from the gurus of Yoga, the heroes of sexual banality squat, not contemplating their navels, but staring in deep concentration at their sexual organs. These men, widely reviewed literati and the others of their ilk, posture like profound pundits while they describe to us with all the grace and beauty that four-letter words permit how they defecate, how they urinate, how they masturbate, how they copulate, how they buggerate, how they fellatiate and how they cacophagate.

Literature

Most books aren't worth the eye-strain.

:-:

There are confidence men in literature as well as in finance, business and politics.

:-:

The worst thing that ever happened to writing is that it became a business. The purpose of business is to make money, and to achieve that end it is necessary to please as many people as possible, to amuse them, to entertain them—in short, to do everything that will help increase the volume of sales.

:-:

A book occurs when man experiences things of great depth and significance and feels compelled to relate his inner experiences. There are such books, written ones as well as unwritten ones.

:-:

If only those would write who have something to say, many who should only watch would get off the field.

Live
As you want to be remembered.

Logic
Man's principles of logic, the fundamental categories of his thinking processes, are universal and identical, not only in today's world, from nation to nation, race to race, group to group, and sex to sex, but also historically. The

structure of civilized man's thinking apparatus of the past and of tomorrow, as far as we can analyze documents and actions, is the same. We could not live together with our fellow citizens for a single day without confusing or even destroying each other were this not the case.

Loneliness
Even the gods would be lonely without man's myrrh and liturgy.

:-:

Loneliness is rare and peculiar company.

Longevity
Even the fleeting butterfly has an infancy, adolescence, middle age and senescence. Perhaps a select few live a bit beyond their three score and ten hours.

:-:

It is less important to prolong the life of the average man than to better his way of living while he is still around.

Love
In love as in religion only those who share the little rituals stay together.

:-:

If only man would stop loving humanity and deity and begin to love just himself—not that in himself which is on the lowest level of man, but rather that in himself which occupies the highest rung.

:-:

The word "love" belongs in that small group of general terms that is used more frequently to disguise an intent or a thought than to divulge it. And if "love" is used in combination with "humanity," the word becomes the most dangerous befogger of them all.

:-:

To love people is to know them.

:-:

There is a lover even for a crab.

:-:

Love is the passion of grief. Amid all the sunlight of affection, there falls the shadow of life rushing away.

:-:

All men love themselves, but some also hate the rest of the world.

:-:

Hate comes naturally, love is to be learned.

:-:

Love may be so ethereal that the presence
of the beloved may reduce the state rather than
increase it. Still, love is no more than the wish
to be together.

Love is the desire to be together, and no
more. Whoever sends his beloved away has long
ceased to love, no matter how reluctant he may
be to admit it. Sometimes nostalgic tremors
may linger on after the beat of love has been
stilled.

:-:

There are some words that need to be broken
up, such as "love." There should be different
terms for the lust to mate and for man's heartful
devotion to kin, friend or God.

:-:

When Messalina seduced a new slave into her
bedroom, she called it love; when King David
heard of the death of Jonathan, he cried out,
"I loved thee more than this earth understands"; when a lecherous roué marries his
latest child-bride, he quakes, "I love you";
when the prophet Isaiah fell under the dagger

of the assassin, he is said to have shouted, "Jerusalem, I love thee!"

If love is of Isaiah, it fits not Messalina. It is a poor banner indeed that serves the knight and the highwayman, and if it stands for crime and seduction, it does not grace issues sanctified by supreme devotion, loyalty, kinship and sacrifice.

:-:

No one can love his enemies unless he first makes them his friends.

:-:

As the African said to the missionary, "Spare me your love, give me equality."

:-:

Our Methodist and Baptist preachers run all over Africa trying to get the black man into their church; right here, where their seminaries are, they work equally hard to keep him out.

:-:

I hate to use the words "united in love." I hate that word "love." It has been so grossly abused for so long a time.

For love of Christ, people were tied to blocks of iron and burned as you would not burn a chicken, living and trembling; for the love of

Allah, captives' hands were cut off so they could no longer serve infidelity; for the love of Jupiter, Roman slaves' tongues were cut out because they spoke unholy prayers. For the love of racial purity, churches were bombed and children lynched.

"Love" is a sinful word. It permits the evildoer to go about his deviltry with a quiet conscience, since all his deeds are done out of "love." What a dastardly confusion of reality.

Love is as love does.

:-:

Love is the grand executioner. It is the grand pretense. When the captains of Henry the Navigator, Prince of Portugal, sailed on their slave hunts to Africa to tear black shepherds and peasants from soil and family and send them into slavery, on their banner was written *"Pro amore Dei"*—"For the love of God." The daggers of Hitler's elite SS officers bore the legend "For love of Fatherland and Führer." And on the platforms upon which the auto-da-fé was performed by Ferdinand and Isabella and a battalion of ecstatic priests, monks and nuns, you can still read the engraving "in humility and love before Christ." Agamemnon put his daughter on the sacrificial block in place of a goat because he loved his Greece. Hindu priests tied the widow to the burning body of the deceased husband because they loved fidelity. And Queen Elizabeth put the Catholic Mary Stuart on the block out of love for the Protestant church, as her own younger sister, Queen Mary, had put four bishops to the torch out of love for Catholicism.

:-:

Some preach love of mankind but cannot love a single human.

:-:

The churches claim to be schools of love; I never met a class that would qualify.

The Reformed Church in South Africa teaches love, the Baptist Church in Alabama teaches love, the Eastern Church in Egypt teaches love, the Catholic Church in Poland teaches love, the Lutheran Churches in Hitler's Germany taught love over love, Sunday by Sunday—but Christ stopped at the church gate. And the love-moist eyes of neither Pope nor Bishops of Italy and Germany could see the gruesome spectacle of daily, weekly, monthly, yearly extermination of the people of Israel.

I presume love is blind.

Loyalty

To trust the erring is generous, to trust the disloyal is weakness.

:-:

To hear some talk, one might think that disloyalty is a privilege and not a villainy.

:-:

Loyalty implies fealty to law and not liege. The man acting out a crime for the sake or at the order of his liege is not loyal but only subservient. When the vassals of the Moravian King Clodovic had blinded, maimed or murdered all his royal relatives, the assistants were not loyal, only unprincipled. The medieval nobility from knight to Kaiser ruled and perished by intrigue and violence, and their heroic epics of noblesse are the tragicomic deception of an uninformed posterity.

Lust

Is lust and has its place, but not as a metaphysics.

Luther

Not a single minister of Luther's church rose up to give the lie to the monstrous accusations against the Jews. In the same breath did they hail Christ as they hailed Hitler. The shame of the German people is the shame of the German church.

Lying

May not be good, but the bare truth is not always a blessing.

Lynching

More people are lynched within the law than ever were outside of it.

M

Machine Age
It has enlarged the possibility of tyranny from a local matter to intercontinental scope.

Malevolence
Rides easily on the tongue; it is the good word that sets heavily in the throat.

Malice
Is not innate but inbred.

Man
Some love nature to the exclusion of man, but he is one of God's creatures, too.

:-:

Men are petrified children. If one would only try to visualize them as they were when children, one's understanding would be easier and one's judgment kindlier.

:-:

No man need be taken seriously who cannot laugh about himself.

:-:

Man is a many-layered creature. It is hard to get him to peel.

Manners
Good manners may require restriction of conversation to pleasantries, but, then again, good manners will not improve the world.

Marriage
Is the only business in which adolescents are permitted to make a contract.

:-:

Marriages may be made in heaven, but people live on earth.

Martyrs
The greatest of them all are in oblivion. They perished long before their cause became victorious, and history honors in the main those who fought and won or those who fell in the last battle.

Marxism
Created dictatorship over the proletariat, not by the proletariat.

Marxist Athena

The Pharaohs of yore claimed descent from the gods: those of today stoutly maintain they sprang directly from the head of Karl Marx.

Masses

No man is so small that he does not consider himself above the masses.

:-:

They say the masses need religion; rather the power-mad leaders need it and need it badly.

:-:

The masses are not those who think but don't know; rather are they those who know but don't think.

Materialism

I suspect the enemies of materialism. They either live off idealism or drape it about themselves like a cloak to keep from being touched by the tears and sweat of the victims of ideologies.

Mathematics

Is the language through which nature speaks to her children—but there is also God, and He is not a mathematician.

Medals

The noncombatant invariably winds up with the largest string of ribbons and medals.

Medical Fallacies

There is hardly a medical fallacy that was not at one time or another "standard treatment." Who knows which of our present "standard treatments" will be the fallacies of tomorrow?

Minds

On guard for the little falsehood often fall prey to the big one.

Memory

To remember the correct date is a gift; to remember the correct principle is a virtue.

:-:

The power of remembering may be a gift, but the power to forget is a blessing.

:-:

Why retain a mental picture of trifles? Only great events are worth remembering.

Mental Cases

Are not the sore spot in this world; it is the

clear-headed minds that are full of schemes marching on the road to power over corpses, rubble and despair.

Mercy
Words of mercy are a bow toward Heaven but deeds of mercy open its gate.

:-:

Mercy is thrice justice.

Midrash
Or the oral interpretation of the Bible has about run its full course and exhausted every possible aspect. We need less exegesis and more emphasis on the true principles of the Old Testament, which can be reduced to a one-page fundamental.

Mind
A glass splinter reflecting a ray of infinite Sun, dreaming of itself as hearth of the universe.

:-:

Mind is an open garden and weeds are plentiful.

:-:

Too much emphasis is given to the mentally deviated and not enough to the mentally corrupted. It is not the neurotics who retard the world's progress, but the ruthlessly ambitious.

:-:

There are some ill-fitting gears in the mental machinery. To most questions we seem to find, or hope for, a corresponding answer, yet there are queries open that foil even an attempt to reply.

:-:

Mind mirrors reality, or only glows like a window reflecting a distant ray—who can fathom this phantom looking glass?

:-:

Mind measures the vastness of galaxies, visible and supposed, and finds it cannot sustain the vision of endless firmament. Endless space and infinite time are just the whisper of a bewildered soul.

:-:

If God is anywhere, He dwells within that heart of hearts raising its eyes to the infinite. God finds Himself in the mind of man; the mind's vision of God is God Himself.

Minority
The student of history knows that the minor-

ity has, often as not, been closer to the truth than the dominant group.

:-:

A minority has no right to govern, but a claim to be respected.

Miracle

Nothing seems to the masses more plausible than the improbable.

They will readily accept a fantastic wonder of the past but, for the present, they will have no miracles.

:-:

Miracles are no proof of saintliness. The Devil performs them too.

:-:

The concept "miracle" is not natural with man. Even primitive man neither hopes nor expects a miracle. He protects himself as well as he can when in danger. And when in danger or in sickness, he will seek help from a neighbor or what he considers an experienced practitioner. There are, of course, many things primitive man does not understand, as there are many things civilized man does not understand. But nothing in the human mind will expect anything like a miracle to solve any issue or problem.

The concept "miracle" or divine intervention in human or natural affairs is not innate in man, but rather imposed upon man by a superstitious clergy or superstitious lay persons who are either victims of the same process or originated these esoteric fabrications with something which mind libertology understands much better today than in antiquity.

The bringing of *deus ex machina* or "the good Lord" from the wings onto the stage of this troubled world as a temperamental healer of sickness; setter of bones; smasher of bridges; giver of fertility; general of war chariots; master over mast and sail; repriever of felony; curer of the blind, deaf and dumb; manipulator of rain, hail and snow; producer of springs, and on occasion trainer of horses—priests and preachers, shamans and medicine men, gurus and mullahs were able thus to bedevil their naive congregations, as well as the folks outside, so that their own position within their respective social structures became quite formidable.

Who would dare to disobey, be he king or beggar, vagrant or native, with the fear of some horrible celestial repercussions?

The naively faithful would reason that the

members of the theological profession, so deeply steeped in holy scholarship, would naturally be living in considerable intimacy with the divine powers, after which they referred to themselves.

The divines who displayed, with doubtful accuracy, studious illustrations of theistic hierarchy—they surely must be under the protection of the divinity they interpret; prayers under their guidance would rise through the proper channels to reach the ear of the immortal saints and the King of the heavens.

It is rather difficult to understand why thinking people would assume that the good Lord can be swayed by genuflecting, by tearful prayers, by ardent appeals, by vows and sacrifices of repentance, and finally by open offers of bribe, like the building of a shrine, convent or church.

If the good Lord helps one sick child, like a good doctor, he will heal all of them. If the good Lord could give one poor, blind man vision, he could give it to all. If He could stop one child from tumbling down the cliff, he could stop all. If He could help one good army to victory, he could bring about the defeat of all vicious aggressors—unless you want to assume that the good Lord is a poor doctor, a poor judge and a poor general. And to think so is rather sinful.

But so peculiar is the human mind set up

that even many of the bright ones are only concerned with their own troubles and care not even to contemplate the tribulations of the others. Wishing in the narrowness of their comprehension their own children to get well, their own armies to reach victory, their own businesses to prosper, their own ships to come in, they attribute to the Almighty such miraculous powers of intervention that if such miracles truly did occur in the manner the egocentric supplicants desire, they would be more the act of the Devil than an act of God.

Mirror

Every once in a while we stop and quickly glance at our friend to find out how we look in his eyes. The rest of the world matters little—it is how our friend reflects our deed that counts. We all live lives except for that mirror.

Misconceptions

A renegade fanatic turns invariably to another dogmatism, rarely to a position of neutral objectivity.

:-:

Men are so steeped in misconceptions, it is easier to lead them into new ones than clarify those they possess.

Misery

Can live without company but joy cannot.

Mismanagement

Openly acknowledged is a sign of democracy; in tyrannies there *seems* to be always perfection.

Missionaries

In Africa and Asia were fighting a losing battle; they treated the natives like children, and the colonials treated them like cattle.

Mistakes

The man who admits his mistakes is better than the sage; he has both wisdom and courage.

A Mob

His many heads, but most often only one cunning brain doing its scheming.

Modernism

Is the belittlement of a splendored past by a dull present.

Mona Lisa

The Mona Lisa reminds me of the barely average Hollywood actress publicized into a fantastic peak of popularity. There are a hundred Renaissance paintings of vastly superior craftsmanship and depth than this portrait by assignment. The people wish to glory in star systems, and in this wish they will raise one thing or another, one person or another, into the heavens. If you look closer, the great are not so tall and the little are not so tiny.

Monasticism

One does not get closer to God by leaving the world. The Shepherd can best be found near to His flock.

Money

Some honor what they lack more than those who possess it.

Monuments

Fortunate for us that the hallowed statues of some exalted personages cannot come to life again.

Moral Philosophy

It is one thing to teach or preach moral philosophy, another entirely to apply it to life under stress.

Morality

Is a set of rules that all men are breaking day in, day out—only some rather noisily.

:-:

Morality is certainly wanting in some respects, but immorality is a poor substitute.

:-:

Morality is the observance of the rights of others. One cannot be immoral but in relation to others. What one does to oneself or with oneself may be wise or foolish, but never immoral. One may abuse his body and yet be respectful of the welfare of others and thus quite moral. And one may discipline his flesh with all precepts of hygiene and asceticism and be a hard, selfish, hurtful person and thus grossly immoral.

It is only in relation to society that man is good or bad, moral or immoral. By himself he may be sober and moderate or very careless, but never good or bad.

:-:

I do not think that abstinence is a way to morality, but goodness is.

:-:

Morality is always the same. However, immorality varies from generation to generation.

:-:

Nothing is immoral that is not meant to hurt

others, and nothing is moral that is meant to do so.

:-:

I have always considered it tactless for the law to walk into people's bedrooms and pontificate there on what one may do with whom and where and when. The function of the law is to safeguard personal security and public welfare. Where no such issues are involved, the law has no business at all, unless called upon by an offended person to protect his or her endangered rights.

Mortality

Is a sobering thought. Unfortunately, it occurs to most people at a time when it is too late to do anything about their lives.

Motivated Thinking

Away from the fields of science and technology, we encounter the great precursor of disagreement: human motivation. Because of it wise men speak like fools and shrewd men utter superstitions. In politics, in religion, in historiography, in anthropology, in jurisprudence, Babel lives again. Every nation speaks a different language. Indeed every person does. This is the great era of motivated thinking and we can almost predict what a man will say once we know to which group he belongs or where his motives lie.

Motivation

Man's inner motivations are quite intricate and complicated; more often than not, there is a combination of motives that shapes the resolves of man, and not a single affection. Underneath all this remains man's subliminal emotional drive for self-preservation that differs in intensity and orientation, but never in direction. Motives are sometimes uncouth and blatant, like those of the Southern White Council member who thinks the Negro is savage, but who actually is in fear of the black man's competition. Motives are sometimes mere ambitious greed, like those of the Southern rabble-rouser who, knowing differently, pursues a line of Negro slander in order to gain an election. Motives may be subtle, like those of a physiologically weak white specimen threatening or assaulting a helpless black man in order to impress his friends or a sexual companion with his prowess. Motives may lie in traditional hatred, inculcated in Southern persons by their elders.

I could go on and enumerate scores of variations in motivation that may, and do, lead to anti-Negro thinking. This method may be applied to similar though slightly different relations between any dominant and minority group. It should not be difficult at all to analyze the thinking of the Germans of the Hitler era or the Ukrainians of the present era in their relationship to the Jewish minority; these two large nations have developed, from a whole set of ugly envy motivations, a Mephistophelian thought-pattern about the Jews which exists nowhere but in their decadent minds.

What has driven their minds into a frightful, morbid corner is not a variation in thinking, but rather a poisoning in their emotional grounding.

Motives

Hold the reins over man's mind.

Mourning

Will not bring back dead heroes, but fulfillment of their plans will give them eternal life.

Museums

I hope to see the day when the portraits of such as Henry VIII or Louis XIV and the other thousands of murderous condottieri hang in museums of criminology and not in public buildings or art galleries. I want to see the picture of Queen Elizabeth I alongside that of Henry Morgan and the other pirates and not alongside Thomas More, the man her father murdered.

Music

The wordless cry of the inner soul reaching for love's fulfillment and beatitude. Beethoven's symphonies, the slow movements: The Lord Himself walks through the silent forests of His domain.

There is another music: the stirring beats of lusty savages, the screech and fury of bored sophisticates jazzing a tired night to death, the whinny of the Devil on the brink of borderline humanity.

:-:

I have often wondered why men write music to poetry and rarely poetry to music. It would be a great and new art to set the symphonies of Beethoven into poetry!

N

Naïveté

Cynical usurpers plied their sardonic wit on the naïveté of the commoners: Alexander named a city after his horse, Bucephalus. Caligula went him one better by appointing his horse, Incitatus, a senator.

Names

Should be assumed, not presumed. The Jews, for instance, were given offensive names by some of their presumptuous Christian neighbors in order to embarrass them.

:-:

Names should be changed to suit men. Some trail ludicrous appendages after them. I have seen giants with names suitable for a dwarf and women with men's names.

:-:

Names should be means of identification and decoration, not embarrassment and confusion.

Napoleon

Napoleon and Alexander killed to conquer; Hitler and Stalin conquered to kill.

Narcotics

Addiction to narcotics is a melancholy sickness but there is no crime in it, only lack of physical and mental hygiene, lack of prudence, lack of foresight. Crime enters the scene in the footsteps of the law. The law creates the crime by its senselessly rigid prohibition, thereby creating a class of narcotics smugglers and pushers whose high prices for delivery of cheap hemp and poppy derivatives overwhelm the people of the street, driving them into the gutter of crime.

Nastiness

Is the tyranny of the peewee.

Nationalism

It is peculiar that nationalistic zealots are not even natives of the countries they allegedly wish to glorify: Alexander was not a Greek, Napoleon not a Frenchman, Hitler not a German, and Stalin not a Russian.

Natural Law

Man is inclined to elevate his hypothetical

explanations of natural phenomena to the status of Universal Laws.

Nature

Who can fathom why nature is so designed that creatures can exist only by destroying other creatures?

:-:

Nature, never wrong, wrongs many.

Nearsighted

To the nearsighted sundown appears earlier.

Negro

Someday a lotion may solve an issue where emotion has failed; a yet-to-be-found chemical will neutralize the dark pigment of our neighbors and leave the many palefaced inferiority complexes stranded on their prejudices.

:-:

If you humiliate one black man, you degrade all the Negroes; if you stone one Jew, you hit all of them.

Negro Baiters

They call on Jesus in the church and on Beelzebub in the street.

Neighbors

One always carries their picture with him, but often it is a caricature.

:-:

Do not bother loving them—just cease hating them.

:-:

What good is all geography, knowing the look of people across the seven seas, if you don't know your neighbor across the yard?

Neurotics

Leave them with us! They are the spice in our bland diet! Leave us Dostoyevski, Paganini, Beethoven! Take not from us the impulsive, faddish, and fantastic, the romantic and illumined poets, the prophets and arty princes lest we remain a race of ordinated zeroes led by rosy-cheeked dullards out of a well-adjusted textbook.

:-:

The American society is hard on the hunt for neurotics, but the great evils in the world are perpetrated by the so-called normals, not the deviates.

In Russia, sober, calculating politicians are keeping millions in concentration camps and are giving a deadly time to their Jewish citizens, for instance, simply in an opportunistic speculation of gaining power in Western Asia. In Red China scores of educators and jurists, following a peculiar brand of socialism, advise the young on how to denounce their parents who do not follow the official party line. Such denunciations invariably end with the elders being publicly executed before the very eyes of grisly, elated, icy youth.

And in our lands, cold-eyed townsmen of the South refuse to convict perpetrators of murder and kidnaping the blacks, while unemotional, shrewd legislators of the White Council stamp rant against basic principles of humanity.

All these and many other sinister elements in our society are the drags that stop humanity from rising to loftier heights, not the unimportant neurotics screwed up in their petty little complexes.

:-:

It is not the neurotic who turns the world

upside-down; it is the level-headed schemer with his tricks of charlatanry.

Neutralism

In the fight between the red and the black, some prefer to remain colorless. If you look hard you may note the yellow showing through.

New Era

A new epoch began with the Nuclear Terror overhanging. We have left the era of incessant wars and entered the period of peaceful animosity.

The New Testament

To the Jews this book is a horror, no less than the *Protocols of Zion* or *Mein Kampf*.

It matters not that this work holds some of the finest passages in religious literature. The Jew, in that novella, has assigned to him the sign of the Devil incarnate. The Jew Christ is painted golden and white, all goodness and divinity—the rest of His people are pictured bearing the mark of Cain, patriarch of the sons of hell. As in *Mein Kampf* the Jew is the sinister offspring of a race of congenital sinners.

Such teachings made it easy for Christians of all times to torture, bleed, cut, garrote, and burn the Jews, even their infants, their sick and old.

And such teachings made the Christian feel guiltless in ignoring Hitler's massacre of a million little children who had done no wrong except to belong to the race whereof Jesus was born.

Christ's family descendants, his own kin and his mother's kin, perished in the holocaust of Christian Germany that made the Protestant churches jubilant collaborators, the Vatican a partner in concordat, and Von Papen, Hitler's mentor, an honored councilor of the Holy See.

May Christ forgive them for gassing the infants of His people, I cannot.

The Christians lack the original Canon of their faith. All they have is a Greek translation of it. The original Hebrew and the Aramaic are extant. Jesus spoke no other tongue.

News

Is not what you read today but what happened today.

Night

Is perhaps a reminder to us that our globe orbits in the dark of space.

Nirvana

Even when it comes to steps of perfection, some priests have an urge to number them.

Nobility

The psychoanalyst wants you to do the smart thing, God wants you to do the noble thing. Where do you wish to make your place, on the couch or in history?

:-:

Nimbus rises not from a calloused palm or a belabored brain, but from a gentle heart.

Notoriety

In our society notoriety differs from fame only in that the latter is of shorter duration.

Oath

The offhand remark of an honest man is better than the oath of a weakling.

Obedience

To the rule of the tyrant is nothing but rationalization by the moral slave.

Oblivion

Is not the enemy of the great; rather do their false and fanciful disciples place them in the shade.

Obscurity

Scratch the obscure and you find a simple man.

Old Age

It is a pity that modern society desires to expel its senior citizens from active life by relegating them to islands of hobbying and childish leisure preoccupations.

Playgrounds for oldsters with their pretended frolicking are only deserts of loneliness, just as the so-called old-age homes are anything but homes.

This process of exile of the old from living society is no better than the expulsion among primitive tribes of the aged to the isolation of the distant jungle.

Old people don't wish to be among the old, just as ill people don't wish to live among the sick.

:-:

Stars that have been ignored all morning, noon and evening open up in the late of the night to brighten the hours of the lonely wakeful.

:-:

As you get closer to the end, the "big things" of life lose their size and the little things loom bigger and bigger.

:-:

Happy the man who gains sagacity in youth, but thrice happy he who retains the fervor of youth in age.

Old People

A house without young people has its windows to the back yard; a house without old people left its foundation in the gutter.

Opinion

The great obstacle to truth is the common man's lethargic reluctance to make a thorough house-cleaning of his mind.

Opportunism

Is the greatest barrier to progress.

:-:

There are two ways of looking at the world and there are two ways of leading one's life: to do what is right, or to do what is opportune. By this proposition there are two types of persons, opportunists and the right kind.

:-:

How many rush to the support of the strong when the weak are in distress!

Opposition

Some splash in it as if by saying nay you have already solved all crises and issues.

Optimism
Is a devil-may-care hope born out of the fear
to face hard truths.

:-:

Optimism may change your mood, but nothing else.

:-:

Optimism can be a matter of philosophy as
well as disposition.

Orator
Being great in rhetoric without profound
calling or message is like being adept in stage
fencing—without purpose or honor to the
rapier.

Oratory
The magic quality of making a trickle thunder like a torrent.

Original Sin
If Adam had not eaten the apple, what would
the Christians have done for theology?

Originality
The original mind knows best how much of
an eclectic he is.

Orthodoxy

No one is more insufferable on rigidity of observance than the man who has nothing else.

:-:

Orthodoxy with many is purely pretentious or nostalgic, like the meat-eater belonging to a vegetarian society.

Others

What makes you think you look better to others than they look to you?

Our World

God is in His heaven and the Devil on earth.

Overlordship

Was once established by the strong fist, then by the keen blade, and now by the sharp tongue.

P

Pain

Pain is always a fanged serpent, but to the fearful it has a hundred heads.

Paradise

Is nowhere, but peace can be had anywhere.

:-:

How can the heavens be glorious, happy and serene while this earth is full of grief and bitterness?

Passing

You shall not live your years again, so treasure them hour by hour.

Passion

Is given to prophets as well as to sinners.

:-:

Passion is no sin; history is alive with dispassionate enemies of humanity.

266 |

Past

Our known past is but a brief paragraph in the book of time.

Patience

Is out of place in the quicksand.

Patriotism

So many of the great patriots were and are men of age. Men whose lives are flowing away caress the beloved nation of which they are a part. It is in the love of his people that mortal man never dies.

:-:

Patriotism is too often not an attitude but a profession.

:-:

The patriot is not the one who loudly praises his own; he is just a braggart. A patriot is the man who praises the land and the people that are dedicated to freedom and brotherhood.

Peace

Loud talk about an allegedly desired peace is a common device to disarm the victim before attack.

:-:

The Caesars were in the habit of vehemently pleading for peace whenever they planned an attack against a quiet neighbor.

:-:

Peace is possible only when the law is greater than men. The tragic situation is that in most lands there are still people who are greater than the law.

:-:

Submission to tyrants makes not for peace but unending war.

:-:

Peace with the Devil remains a one-sided arrangement.

:-:

Even an angel could not live in sanctity with the Devil about.

:-:

The people of today are as peaceful as they ever will be, but still there are hangmen at the helm of state. The warmongers of our time do not thunder from shaggy horses—they are doctors of philosophy like Mao, theologians like Stalin, schoolteachers like Mussolini, painters like Hitler, or jolly organizers like Khrushchev. But they have bled to death more men and women than the malefactors of all the past generations put together.

:-:

Those who warn of war invariably shout of peace and security, and never was a neighbor puny enough not to have frightened the giant at the border into aggression.

:-:

The more a dictator talks of peace, the closer he is to war.

Pedagogy
Went a-traveling to many far places, but bloodshed remained at home—fat, red, ugly as ever.

:-:

If one learns in school to be self-centered, success-greedy, prize-snatching, merit-hogging, one is not likely to become a self-effacing, cooperative member of society.

If one learns in school to be an apple polisher, an errand seeker, an eye catcher, a sleeve brusher, one will have had expert training in sycophancy. If one learns in school to report the cribbing of fellow students while covering up one's own, the lasting lesson has been brought home that snitching is an accepted way of life, stool-pigeoning a duty. The crime of denunciation assumes the shape of a virtue; and there is no sin if you beat the rap.

In schooling where success is noisily crowned Queen of Achievement and covered with the purple of "A" report cards, principals' gold cards and deans' favorite listings, those who get near the crown live in dread of runners-up and in hopeful excitement of getting there ahead of the others—which makes for envy, false pride, and other evil emotions that deface the Lord's image on which man should model his own.

For a principle of morals that could truly serve all humanity bent on betterment, I should like to paraphrase the old Hebrew adage: "Walk in humility and with an outstretched hand."

They don't teach you to walk in humility with an outstretched hand in these schools of ours. Indeed, I would say if it's possible to reverse this maxim, it could well serve as a motto for present-day pedagogy.

:-:

In all their rush for scientific astuteness, our educators seem to have lost sight of the ultimate pedagogic goal: the knowledge of living a good life.

Pens
Too many push a pen who should wield a broom.

People
Whoever loves not his people, loves not God. The Lord made the covenant with a nation, not an individual.

:-:

Perhaps the people are as gullible as the charlatans seem to prove.

:-:

You can't remake all people, but you can manage to avoid some of them.

:-:

The voice of the people is seldom their own.

:-:

One can live in a city a lifetime and not be aware of some of its choicest parts; one can know people a lifetime and not know the best in them.

:-:

Much of the world's population cannot verbalize its discontent. But you can feel their anguish breathing from every pore.

Perception
Of all new people, events and ideas takes place on the used film of our brain; even a brand-new picture registered by our mind is distorted or blurred by the thousand faded prints already on our memory.

:-:

We cannot hear the thunder of the galaxies churning through endless space, nor the whisper of the neutrons colliding in the atom world; there is so very little our ears can register or our eyes behold.

:-:

How frail is man. The thunder of the earth rushing through aeons of time we cannot hear; the billions of planets in cosmic distance we cannot see; and perhaps the great thoughts of creation and the infinity of space we cannot think.

Perfection
The perfect man is not one without faults,

rather, one burdened with all sins and blessed
with the will to overcome them.

:-:

To the ant, its hill may be a perfect world;
to the rest, it's just another bit of sod.

:-:

Most people consider themselves pretty perfect. If they were allowed to appear again in a
revised edition, very few, I venture to say,
would have serious revisions to make of themselves.

Perfidy

A hundred prayers of the Roman Church in
the spirit of divine charity are shot through
with debasing references to the perfidious Jews,
as they call them. Where does charity begin
and where perfidy?

Persuasion

Is a privilege of democracy and the weapon
of tyranny.

Pessimism

Consoles itself with its inevitable sorrow even
as optimism with its inevitable joy, and the rest
of the world may whistle for its salvation.

:-:

Pessimism is the twin sister of optimism, flee-ing into the bleak vastness of the mind in head-over-heels flight from the field of action.

Pets
So long as there is a suffering waif starving in this bitter world it is a sin to cater to a dog.

Philanthropy
Is no evidence of faith, but indifference is proof of itself.

:-:

Watching public benefactors is an embarrass-ment to the indifferent; they will steadfastly belittle the motives of the donors, having them-selves no motive at all.

Philistines
They give such little answers to such big questions.

Philosophers
Are amazed at what most people take for granted.

:-:

The world is full of peacock philosophers

who forever are preoccupied with their own feathers.

:-:

Philosophers and opossums have the habit of looking occasionally at the world upside down. It is a surprising experience.

:-:

It's not knowing yourself that makes a philosopher, but rather knowing your fellow man.

:-:

It may be that the most profound philosophers of all have never uttered a blessed word about what moved them most deeply.

:-:

Philosophers, historians and theologians of the past need be re-examined as to the position they took on the great issues alive in their times.

Those who are listed in our literature as pathfinders of culture let us investigate to see if they were battling eagles or mere crows on the morning after.

Seneca wrote pretty essays on the moral life, but was in his practice the exchequer of bloody Nero; Augustinus lectured in Milan on the equality of man before God, but in his apologetics defended slavery as a God-ordained institution; Thomas Aquinas carried the halo of angelic wisdom, but like most Dominicans had only disdain for the accursed kinsmen of Jesus. I could go on for a whole book to enumerate so-called great who were evil and small, whose nimbus would be put in the shadow by a mere candle of light.

It is time to take the hood off some of the saints who were beatified, canonized and sanctified when the canon was interpreted by despots of the scepter or despots of the tiara.

Philosophy

Is a queen in exile, having lost her entourage but not her regal demeanor, hoping that someday her prodigal servants will return disillusioned with themselves.

:-:

Hesitancy is the beginning of philosophy, and charity its end.

:-:

It is the ability to hesitate before forming an opinion that makes the difference between a philosopher and, shall we say, a parroty mind. Snap judgments are like fishing nets cast with great flourish and prematurely hauled in. A lot of seaweed and broken shell may come up, but hardly any fish.

:-:

Philosophy is either a way of life or a mere figure of speech.

:-:

Philosophy deals with man, not books.

:-:

Philosophy can never be defined because it is the search for the indefinable.

:-:

All man's world is in man's mind; man's mind *is* man's world.

To the timeless universe coursing through infinite space, what it all this but the dreams and doodlings of a blade of grass in the evening wind?

That which man calls "beauty"—what is it? That which man calls "moral"—what is it? What he calls "heritage"—what is it? The blade of grass is singing in the wind and it thinks the wide, wide universe hearkens.

Still man must live as if his world were real and perennial, but if he finds his true and tiny measure, a better man he may be—more humble, more kind, more forgiving, more hesitant.

:-:

Philosophy is the Cinderella of the sciences; she does not even possess her own definition. But once in a generation or so the fairy prince gallops up and raises her high to the castle in the sky.

:-:

Philosophy, like all true friends, will show up best in times of adversity.

:-:

Philosophy is no more than man's orientation in the cosmos, and from this orientation stem the kindness, tolerance, and generosity which are the basis of all true teaching. Beyond these simple tasks of ethics there is nothing that falls in the realm of philosophy.

Philosophy is ethics, or it is nothing at all.

:-:

Logodaedaly is perhaps the greatest threat to philosophy. The inclination to the creation and pursuit of word labyrinths has beclouded the living problems of ethics from Aristotle to Husserl.

Piety

The heartbeats of the Lord are a pulse of harmony, a pulse of love. Are you listening?

Pity

Is where man meets God in fellow man.

Pius XII

History has already uncovered Pope Pius XII as representative of almost unbelievable clerical indifference to human suffering. There lacks a shred of evidence to becloud the tragic spectacle.

At the root of Pope Pius's refusal to utter even a secret appeal to the Nazi government to cease the choking and gassing of a million children of the race of Jesus and five million unarmed adults, there lies not only indolence but total lack of faith in Divine Providence. Cardinals, bishops and scholars appealed to the Vicar of Christ to save the Church from perennial disgrace, but the Pontiff had little faith in the final victory of God over Hitler.

He was concerned with only one thing when they dragged Jews from Rome to Auschwitz: who has the stronger battalions? He saw the power of Hitler. He did not see God, not at all.

Planting

The man who plants a tree does not expect to lie in its shadow.

Pleasant

There is nothing more irritating than unpleasant things said in a pleasant manner.

Pleasures

Can be found where you least expect them.

:-:

There can be as much joy in helping along as in tripping up.

Poet

Sing not a song of disappointed love, it matters only to you; sing not a song of trees and birds and meadowlands, they will not respond; sing not a song of God, His Son and dreamlands in the sky; the gods gave us up long, long ago, turning to far eternities. But sing a song of bitterness, of man's bestiality with man, of vicious demagoguery and hateful purposes against the weak, the innocent and much abused.

Sing a song to freedom or hang your harp on the tree and let the winds send out life's somber melodies.

Poetry

What enchanting webs of sentiment are spun by the poets about such trivial props as the

moon (a bit of burned out stone), the clouds
(a loose volume of steam) and the blossoms
(leaflets decaying above the sprouts of some
weed).

:-:

Poetry: Language of the wounded soul.

:-:

Whispering melody from the faraway shores
of man's pained soul, true poetry is ever melancholy. Plato named it a mania. Is that why every
fifth one of the great bards lived or died in
broken mind?

:-:

Poetic license does not extend to politics.

:-:

The court poet may ride a gilded charger but
never Pegasus.

:-:

Without rhythm and rhyme is also without
reason.

Politicians
Live off the people, statesmen for them.

:-:

Politicians are never more dangerous than

| 281

when they discover in themselves love for mankind.

Politics

A profession holding out the greatest amount of power for the least amount of training or responsibility.

:-:

Whoever declaims not to care about politics has already taken sides with the rulers in power.

Popes

For a thousand years and more the holy city of Rome was the stamping ground of cardinals and other ecclesiastics who might as well have come out of the wrong end of the Purgatory—and, indeed, Dante had them in mind when he wrote his great *Commedia*. There were Popes presiding as Bishops of Rome whose private lives were blacker and bloodier than the most hideous pages of criminal history. In truth, there were some Princes of the Apostles, like Gregory VII, who were men of considerable dedication and learning, and then again there were others who were too weak to fight evil, or too narrow-sighted to see it.

:-:

Pope Paul VI would not condemn anti-Semitism, only deplore it. Pope Pius XII of the Hitler aegis resolved likewise: Killing Jews is naughty but neither sinful nor a heresy.

Posterity
May also err, and its mistakes are difficult for us to correct.

Potentates
The world has always had those who take on the voice of God, and sound off for themselves —those with the cunning tongues who, in depicting the Lord's celestial abode, never fail to point out their own right of eminent domain in its anteroom.

Poverty
Is no crime, but a short cut to it.

:-:

It is the disgraceful symptom of our whole known era, that forever wastes the people's sweat on the mansions of the rulers, cheapens the price of blood in defense of them, and raises the cost of bread for the expendables.

Only the freedom of tears exists among the masses of Eurasia and Africa. And the princes of Arabia or India, the chieftains of Russia or China, may toss a fortune into armlets or arms while the people perish for want of nourishment.

Poverty is a disgrace, a disgrace to human fellowship.

:-:

Perhaps some poverty will always be with us, but such poverty among so many in the presence of such wealth among so few is incongruous.

:-:

It is not society that owes the poor man a living, it is those within society who have acquired so much of the riches that there is nothing left for some. They owe it to them.

Power

Still comes first in Eurasia's nations, with scholarship a stumbling, rationalizing second. After the ugly deed is done, theory is called in to contrive justification.

:-:

Power is what they seek, the ambitious beetle, ant, or spider—until a careless step by some wandering animal crushes their flimsy web or nest.

:-:

Those lusting for power over the proletariat hide their greed under a cloak of justice for the downtrodden, as the Crusaders camouflaged their yearning for Byzantine riches with the Cross of Suffering.

Praise
Watch out for praise; its twin is derision.

Prayer
Where the heart does not long for love eternal and peace among men there is no communication with the Divine; there is no true prayer. Prayer is the pining of the soul of man for the soul eternal, in this aimlessly drifting world of evil and illness, pain and deceit.

:-:

Those who pray to God for blessings beggar the grace of worship.

:-:

A serene word, a chapel on your lips, if those lips were only for fellow man and fellowship instead of for favors and privileges.

:-:

The Lord knows your needs, what wants revealing are your deeds.

:-:

Pray to your conscience for guidance and not to the Lord for deliverance.

:-:

Compassion is the prayerful solemnity practiced by the truly devout. The truly pious sends out no prayers for himself, only for his fellow creature.

The Hebrew books of wisdom say that only prayers of compassion reach the heaven; all others fall back to earth, being tied to earthly wishes and earthly wants.

:-:

Take a look at the prayer books of the Mohammedans or Hindus, Christians or Buddhists and the many other faiths, minor or major, and you will be startled by the submissiveness of the worshippers, who sound like supplicants before an Oriental, ancient or medieval tyrannical overlord.

They begin their prayers with fulsome praise of the tremendous power of the godhead, continue with expressions of extreme humility and wind up with pitiful appeals for assistance in their various enterprises, protection from troubles or a quick cure for their ailments. In their desire to gain favor in the eyes of Olympus, they ardently confess to failings and sins and even blame their covetous eyes.

:-:

Praying with words, and praying with hands, and praying with bent knees are only remnants of pagan idolatry. What matters are prayers in deep resolve.

Preachers

Some preachers talk as if they had God in their pocket, while in fact they never even met Him.

Preaching

Is like delivering an ambassadorial message: it is the King's voice that should prevail and not the messenger's fancy.

Prejudices

To have them is natural; to act by them is barbaric.

There is no smugger contentment than being safely surrounded by one's prejudices.

:-:

Logic is ever so often the handmaiden of prejudice.

:-:

Nothing is better established than prejudice, hatefulness and superstition, and nothing sounds more convincing than an old lie.

:-:

The prejudiced will only know what his fellow man lacks, not what he possesses.

:-:

Superstition and prejudices of distant lands and times are readily apparent. It is those close by that are difficult to discern.

:-:

Prejudices cling most readily to the very young and the very old.

:-:

Prejudices seem to have some sort of birthright in the mind: they are there before enlightenment.

:-:

Only the sagacious gain in wisdom as their years go by. The dullard ages not in understanding but in prejudices.

The Press

Should be free but not loose.

Pride

Is a virtue if it is the measure of one's own nobility. It renders itself a sin when its intent is to make others appear ignoble.

Prisons

There must be a better way of re-educating offenders than herding them like unruly cattle into a pen.

Prodigies

An analysis of the great scientists of modern times bears out the fact that the percentage of so-called prodigies among them is basically the same as that among the so-called common people. Quite a few of the most outstanding men of modern history, such as Einstein, Edison, Pasteur, Leonardo da Vinci, Voltaire, Copernicus, Newton, were mediocre students and were completely overshadowed in boyhood days by contemporary "prodigies" who fell by the wayside as the years went on.

Progress

Mankind's speed has quickened but our track is still the very same circle.

:-:

In the last hundred years we have been going two steps forward and three steps backward.

:-:

Tribes used to call each other by beating on tree trunks, then by scratching on clay tablets and paper, and now via electrons.

Still, after thousands and thousands of years, the text of the message has not changed: tribe trafficking with tribe to destroy other tribes.

Proof

You can't prove anything where interest dominates reason.

Property

There should be no debtors' prisons any longer, nor debtors' gallows. If the rich take property, it should be taken back from them; if the poor take property, they should make restitution as well as they can. No man should be put through the torture of incarceration because of inability to make such restitution.

In my eyes, the duty of the law is not to protect property but to protect people.

:-:

It seems the eyes of the law can overlook almost any misdeed and misdemeanor—the maltreatment of minorities, the degradation of the weak, the oppression of the aged, ill and poor, the encouragement of gambling and alcoholism, the corruption of youth by display of the underworld in print and film. The law can overlook a thousand crimes of exploitation, if concocted with care by schemers and scoundrels, but the law has a sharp eye for any offense against property.

The Prophet
Knows no more than ordinary man but he knows it earlier.

:-:

Very few, blessed few, pin their faith directly on the word of God. Most ordinary people anchor their beliefs in other mortals who link God to them. The Hebrews called these prophets *nebiim*, "interpreters."

Prosperity
Is as often the midwife of generosity as of arrogance.

Protesters
Some of them carry on not out of love for mankind but out of disdain for all established society.

Proverbs

Much cherished wisdom of Western philosophers was, millennia before, folk wisdom in other continents.

:-:

Proverbs are the mirror of a people. If we read the proverbs of the Sumerians or Israelites, ancient as the sands of the desert, we begin to realize how little we have added in all the thousands of years to their wisdom of life.

Providence

Is childishly anthropocentric wish-thinking that the winds will change course to blow a dust particle off a petal.

The Prude

Is closer to sin than the indifferent; in fact, the former is ever on the brink of it.

Prudence

May fill the purse but empty the heart.

Psychoanalysis

Hanging a Greek tag on every quiver of human emotion may create the illusion of knowledge where there is only classification.

:-:

Psychoanalysis: The attempt to cure aberrations of the present day by recalling aberrations of the past.

:-:

Mind bespeaks itself. One who finds his milieu a forest of sexual symbols reveals more the status of his own brain than that of his environs.

:-:

Psychoanalysis has added many new words to our language but no new insights.

:-:

Dreams are the play of a drowsy mind; only fools and children take a game for real.

Psychosomatics
Many illnesses originate in the mind; the body lives correspondingly. The problem is: which came first, the inside of the shell or the outside?

Publishing
Much, so very much, of the writing in the Humanities is delimited by the authors' professional interests; indeed, little of it is free.
The college professor in his writings is

"guided" by the expectations, if not require-
ments, of his profession. "Publish acceptable
material or perish" is not entirely a baseless
pronouncement. The clergyman in his sermons
as in his papers has initially, in taking the cloth,
accepted denominational conformism.

The political writer, under the aegis of his
party, will almost automatically gauge events
by platform directives.

Still, among the tons of tedious, biased, un-
inspired and downright opportunistic printed
leaves, one can occasionally come across an un-
tarnished page written for no other purpose
but the sending of an intellectual message from
one man to other men.

Punishment

Habitual criminals should be punished with
compulsory labor which they dread far more
than compulsory idleness.

:-:

Punishment is not the answer to the problems
of crime; it answers only the call for revenge.

:-:

Should be fitted not to the crime but to the
criminal.

Pupils

What good is a literature which excludes the black man, or a religion which keeps him outside its church, or a sociology which tolerates ghettos for Negroes, or a whole damned school that segregates pupils by pigment?

Purity

The water carrier is not necessarily the cleanest man in town.

Q

Questioning
What is of importance to man is not a great body of information but a great body of questioning.

Questions
A thousand questions can be posed off the beaten path; even correct replies will lead nowhere.

R

The Rabbi

Speaks of the Sages and the Sages speak of God. You cannot place a statue on the bare ground, you need a pedestal. The rabbis are the pedestal. It is a thankless lot to have chosen. They serve to enhance the greatness of the Masters and the best they get is to be overlooked.

Race

God cannot see the marks and markings by which humans distinguish themselves from others. He can but see the humans.

:-:

A thousand things distinguish man from man, but only one distinguishes man before God—his conscience.

:-:

Little people make much of the little which makes them different from another, but to the aeons eternalizing the universe, man differs from man as barely as a dust grain varies from a dust grain.

:-:

How little do we know of man's past and how much do we make of that little we know.

:-:

Race is good when taken as an obligation, evil when taken as a privilege.

:-:

If each race were human, there would be only one.

Racism

Racism lives on borrowed time.

The next generation or two will indubitably bring about a chemical discovery that will enable so-called colored people to change their pigmentation almost as effectively as the process now used alters the color of our hair, only more thorough-going and of a more permanent character.

Readers

We have acquired a new class of readers of late, and rather a determined group—if one can still delimit them by this nomen—the literary voyeur, the literary "Peeping Tom." We are no longer dealing with a small shameful embarrassed clan of pornographic devotees but rather with bold-faced men and women who expect their Muses and their Apollo to behave like a Montmartre streetwalker and her pimp. They point to good old Dr. Freud, whose roving fantasies carried him from one aberration through the broad fields of homosexuality, incest, transvestism and self-abuse, over the catharsis of uninhibited genital concentration to the Olympus of ego-nothingness. A man, by his own confessions sex-limited at the age of forty, endeavoring with grand metaphysical gestures to explain to the rest of the world the mysteries of subconscious sex impulses and their derivatives! From embryo to senility a chain of aberrations is clumsily covered up by social inhibitions and crude oppressiveness of day-to-day awareness.

Perhaps the reference to the sex-beclouded Olympus is only a handy philosophical excuse for our new class of literati to peek through the keyhole and broaden the scope of spiritual crotch inspection from the psychoanalyst and sex analyst into a general mode of culture.

One thing is certain, that the last few decades

have reduced much of what appears in books, plays and films to a more or less subtle array of titillating and quite often rather coarse performances in sexual deviations.

Writers obtain sudden repute and of course quite popular sales by semi-confessional fictionals describing in detail, very much in detail, how they were seduced by a twelve-year-old stepdaughter or how they watched the cook and the maid engage in Lesbian frivolities; how they managed successfully to infiltrate a whole school of fags; how a gardener manipulated the anatomical peculiarities of the lady of the house; how a bordello queen indulged in her courtesanship; how a brother would make his sister take notice of him as a man.

All these things and many more, far too involved by the fantastic imagination of the pornographer's pen, have existed throughout known history in human, animal and plant life, but it fell to our generation to become the great harbinger of pornography, not as a furtive back-door script, but rather as front-page parlor literature.

It is a new phase in which the mushroom of pornography has left its basement bed and in almost science-fiction manner broken through the door of the living room and even entered the library and the chapel.

We have hundreds of college professors today from whose lips the words penis and vagina, fellatio, etc., flow ex-cathedra as easily as Homer, Pindar and Plato, and we hear clergymen use the pan-sexual vocabulary of the pornographers with greater ease than the termini of the classic scholars and the reformers as well.

Having had the privilege of meeting personally some of the French and American creators of the new fiction with its exhibitionist flair, I cannot help but feel a certain disdain in imagining these cunning, slovenly, aging daydreamers of orgiastic vintage taking the place of stag-party call girls in lewd performances.

To be frank, I was never offended by the antics of professional stag-party performers. I was rather surprised by the great number of people watching and the slender excuses made to justify these shows.

What I resented most, however, were the ridiculous attempts on behalf of the entrepreneurs as well as critical representatives of the audience to interpret this burlesque as a legitimate show of artistic merit.

Reason

If man be rational then I don't know the meaning of reason.

:-:

The semblance of reason is often more attractive than reason itself.

Rebuttal

Silence is the argument of the sage.

Recluse

To make nothing of the world will not enrich the Heavens and leave the world as poor as ever.

Recognition

Many of the renowned personages did not push the world forward, rather only in circles. They were recognized because that was what they were striving for: recognition. They were less interested in the betterment of the world than in the betterment of their status within the world. They were way out front, but they carefully watched the dominant trend. Those who really pushed mankind forward often did so at the expense of their own comfort, security and even life.

Historians are apt to credit progress to the man up front, not to the man behind pushing.

Reform
Is seldom effective without a dose of reaction.

Reformers
I disdain the reformer who sends youngsters on flimsy boats riding the stormy seas of civil strife while he pontificates on shore.

Regret
Redress is needed, not regret.

Reincarnation
May be true, but I do hope that some who have passed away never come back again in any shape or form.

Religion
Not all religions are good, but there is good in all religions.

:-:

Man's religion is accidental but his faith is not.

:-:

Perhaps all of it can be defined in the admonition to offer your fellow man the first cut of bread.

:-:

Man is generally unaware that the most compelling reason for his clinging to religion is not so much an awareness of divine providence, the ways of which are certainly more confusing to him than satisfying, but rather his intuitive urge to hold on to the sweet mysteries of life.

:-:

Is there a future to religion? Yes, there is—if we take a lesson from our past.

:-:

There are those who suffer from laziness of religious thinking. They do not desire a God whose nature implies their being good to their fellow man—black and white, pagan, Jew, and yellow. They wish a God who is good to them, a God they can pray to for better harvest, for rain, for a quiet sea so their fishing be not impaired. They want a God to whom they can genuflect to heal their sick and bring to life their dead. They want a God of Supplication in favor of fertility and a successful war; they want a God with whom they can strike a bargain for a life hereafter, a good life with featherbeds and fancy living for which they are willing to give coin and candles and sometimes even forego a handsome bit of sex. They want to live forever; and for this "ever" they are willing to pay the price.

Contrary to what some preachers have been telling them, I doubt if Jehovah is ready to make a deal; and if so, I question the desirability of these people in His Realm; and I seriously doubt if the people who pretend to be in His confidence are more than confidence men. There are naïve multitudes who, since time immemorial, have listened to Shaman's admonition not to dare step beyond the prescribed borders of denominational sectdom. These good people, frightened and bewildered, have picked out for themselves a little corner of Shaman tradition, trying to lead a life of religious imitation. They place the fez on their head or a prayer wheel in their hands in their fear of purgatory or their yearning for paradise. They eschew meat on Friday and alcohol the year round. They live on greens and grain and kneel on the prayer rug five times a day. They counted on the ritual since that appeared a sure way to celestial security according to the words of the Shaman. For them, these observances were the Lord's ultimate demands on the road to salvation.

Remorse
Is the gate to ethics, but will carry one no further.

Renaissance
The age of glory was not all splendor; it was simultaneously the era of morbid witch hunts and auto-da-fé. On the other hand the so-called Dark Ages of early medievalism produced in China and Arabia the flowering of art and culture.

Repentance
Repentance is a meaningless gesture often followed by repetition of the offense. The essential thing is self-improvement, not self-demeaning.

:-:

The Catholic Church pronounced with a-plomb: We will no longer call the Jews a for-ever accursed people, although they are the killers of God.

What a noble resolve! We Jews can now breathe freely; our new-borns and infants are without blemish. They carry no devil's horns nor Satan's clubfoot!

Let us thank the learned Cardinals of the Roman Council for this gracious forgiveness, for no longer being publicly maligned by them in pulpit and catechism!

Mind you, O Lord, they are not contrite or despondent for having debased and plagued us for two millennia; nay, the padres are prideful in patronizingly discontinuing *henceforth* their libel.

What curious arrogance!

Repose
Is not the absence of tumult but mastery of it.

Reproof
Is only welcome if its aim is to raise up, not mark down.

Reputation
Is not worth defending, but righteousness is.

:-:

Reputations often travel in opposite directions from their subjects.

Resignation
Perhaps the wisest begin and end their lives

in obscurity, and even in passing, steal away from the rest without an epitaph—unknown giants in a realm of dwarfs.

Resurrection

The breathtaking concept of man's religion, an immortal soul in eternity!—in small eyes, a selfish vision of personal reward in a comfortable hereafter arranged by a police-judge type deity for the goody-goodies.

Retirement

Assigning a man a deathbed as his future living quarters.

Retribution

Is not God's way, but man's wish.

Revenge

Uses the words of justice but the voice is crime's.

Reverence

Those who have no regard for their own dignity will never cherish it in others.

Reviewers

Some forget that they are only heralds and not the heroes of the play.

Reward

Education won for a reward is like love won for a bracelet.

Right

May not always make might, but you'll not find it while on your knees.

:-:

The test of existing rights lies in daily practice, not in abstract constitutions.

Righteousness

It is never too late to start on the path of righteousness, and the road to evil will always be only a step away.

Rights of Man

I would like to see a new era in church activity when the ministers and priests cease their lip service to the phantom word "love" and become standard-bearers in the fight for justice and the rights of man.

:-:

Even if the economic status of the Russian peasant were better than that of the French, or that of the Chinese fisherman better than that

of the British, or that of the Czech worker better than that of the American—Communism in
its stark reality would have to be condemned
because within its far-flung borders there is not
a glint of personal freedom. No human recognition is given to the political opponent, and
not a shadow remains of the right of man to
elect his own representatives. There is no right
to strike, there is no right to voice a grievance
without punishment, there is not even the right
of the condemned to die in his faith.

Ritual
No rite or ritual is essential, but goodness is.

Rivalry
The common habit of "encouraging" students by public shame and public prizes to push
themselves to the front benches may improve
their marks but mark them for life.

:-:

Rivalry is the root of all social evil—and yet
it is nurtured still in our pedagogy.

:-:

The wish to outdo others is a greed, not a
virtue.

Romance

Lives not in the people but in their dreams. Who does not dream will never encounter the greatness of love, daring, adventure and devotion.

Romanticism

So many have expressed the wish to have lived in the great times of such men as El Cid, Alexander or Napoleon. Do these romanticists ever contemplate the feelings of the citizens of Valencia who surrendered upon promise of security to El Campeador only to be slaughtered in the most brutal manner; or those of the Turkish garrison at Joppa who signed an armistice with the Corsican and upon turning in their weapons were summarily arrested, tied to trees twenty at a time and bayoneted to death, all fourteen hundred of them; or those of the citizens of Thebes who refused to offer their sons for the marauding armies of Alexander and thereupon were massacred, ten thousand of them, men, women and children?

These romanticists have sought out for themselves in their daydreams a good seat at the arena. How different do matters appear when you yourself are in the arena.

The world looks mighty glamorous from the

vantage point of Caesar's box, but the masses of the people are not in the box, they are in the bloody sand and dirt of the arena.

Rome

For those who admire the aesthetic aspects of the sundry arches of triumph in Rome, may we spread before them the sordid panorama to which all these art pieces of architecture directly led—arenas where men, women and children of a hundred European and Asian nations were pressed into a sanguinary circus for what is called "the glory that was Rome," which in truth was blood and blasphemy.

Royal Privilege

It is immoral to accept persons as being of high social status because one of their ancestors was a queen's lover or a queen's pirate, a king's henchman or a king's straw boss over miserable serfs. There is a stench to these royal privileges, the stench of dungeon, double dealing, bondage, poverty and misery.

Royalty

Somewhere on every royal coat of arms should be engraved an executioner's ax.

:-:

Royalty used to carry a scepter, now it sports a vodka bottle.

Russia
The land where the accused knows the verdict before the jury.

:-:

The Soviets have all but conquered illiteracy, yet in the excitement of the campaign they mislaid The Book.

S

Sabbath

Is not sanctified by abstention from work, but by devotional attention.

:-:

God gave you six days, give Him one!

:-:

They call the Sabbath the poor man's day. There will come a time when all seven will belong to him.

Sages

I do not deny the life hereafter, but I do not think it is for sale. I do not deny the mercy of the Lord, but I doubt if prayers can arouse it or blasphemy can still it.

Sages are not the men who improvise proverbs for posterity but those who take a stand

in their own time against the evil then prevalent.

Saint

The Biblical Hebrew language has no word
for saint. In the eyes of the Hebrew prophets
all men are sinners, all men remain sinners.
Moses was a sinner, and so were Solomon and
David and all the other leaders who were the
makers of the sacred scriptures and texts. But
they were more than sinners. They were imbued with the spirit of *zedikah,* justice, a term
which has served many of the great teachers as
a synonym for God. God is Justice, God is
charity, God is compassion, but man is forever
a sinner who may be imbued with *Shechinah,*
the spirit of justice, charity or compassion; man
is never a saint or saintly.

Salvation

To many, Jesus is an alibi not a savior.

:-:

Socrates has no followers because his testament was that salvation must be earned by every
man for himself. Jesus' flock runs into millions
because He took pains of salvation upon Himself.

Sanctity

Sitting in the front pew brings you no closer to God.

Sanctity of Life

Is a great principle to uphold but greater yet is that of the dignity of man.

:-:

Sanctity of life is a noble but inconsequential attitude. The ankle bell of the Hindu, which sends out warning to whatever crawls of the crushing threat of his feet, sounds gentle enough, but besides the millions of ticks and worms that draw their life from the skin and blood of man, there are billions of minutely tiny beasts infesting man's arteries and tissues that must be poisoned so man may live. Holy only is the life of no sin; much of the animal life that crawls and flies is a curse to man and a disease.

Satan

To the devils Satan appears quite respectable.

Savage

The white man kills more neatly, not less.

School

Youth has a right to be regarded as a goal and

not as a means. In a free society every boy and girl has a right to live a young life of self-respect and respect without comparison to others, be they better or worse, more clever and adept or less cunning and diligent. If a teacher cannot deal with the young but by the whip of threats and the bribe of rewards, he is as little fit to sit under the blackboard as a judge with such a frame of mind would be fit to sit on the bench.

Every boy and girl has a right to have his or her natural gifts of body and mind tended to, be they great or small, as individual talents, without being driven to demoralizing contests for scholastic rewards, without being subjected to the dehumanizing effects of shabby victories over classmates and equally dehumanizing humiliation of alleged failure. It is easy to deal with pupils, whip in one hand and honey in the other. Labor used to be dealt with in the very same way, but the time has come to drop the sorry tradition of competitive schooling as the time came generations ago to drop the tradition of competitive labor management.

The praise and rewarding of the gifted and diligent is as demoralizing as the public criticism of the less endowed and less patient, because the goal of education does not lie in the subject, but rather in the student. It isn't what you put into the student that matters so much as what you bring out of him. You may pour into his brain with Nuremberg funnel all the seven wisdoms, up to the rim; if you can't get out of him the spark of human kindness and the yearning to raise the standards of mankind in a life of co-operation, you may have gained him a whole array of honors and medals, but you have rendered no service to youth and society.

:-:

School is the place where family prejudices are replaced by public ones.

:-:

There seems to be time in all our schools for sports and frills and recreation, but none for the study of ethics.

:-:

We seem to find it necessary in our schools to teach a variety of languages—not enough to know, just enough to forget; we teach the lives of the kings and generals, the diplomats and the court clerks and camarillas, which should be reserved for those who take an interest in political criminology; we teach the youngsters a hundred names of leaves and other particles of plants they will never see, while they can't distinguish an apple tree from a cherry tree and don't know if lemons grow on a bush or a branch; we teach them the names of a thousand bones of frogs and fishes and sundry other creatures, adding only to the great body of useless information acquired in school and promptly left there at graduation.

The most important subject, however, *how to get along with fellowmen*, is left to chance and worse.

:-:

Students are people and should be left to lead their lives without constantly being compared with others and forever being rated against the accomplishments of others, and without being relentlessly pushed to outdo their peers and reach for the top.

And, pray tell me, what is on the top? A brilliant physicist working in a Russian laboratory on nuclear weapons? An astrophysicist in Hitler's rocket center calculating how to bombard London? A Chinese bacteriologist figuring out how to spread a plague over America through a series of little bombs? A sociologist in an Alabama university preparing a learned resolution as to why Negroes are not entitled to sit on a bench next to a member of that sallow race that chooses to call itself white? That legal pundit in Little Rock who contrives ways and means of using the law to block justice?

What is on top that is worth destroying the life and dignity of young people to get there?

:-:

So many boys and girls have I seen pass their school years in an aura of glamour, bemedaled and behonored. I tried to follow, for my purposes, their trek, and I found so many of them a sorry lot in later life.

They had learned much in their school years, and as they were gifted with certain proficiencies of memory and quick attention, they excelled in the classroom. But much of what they had acquired turned out to be ill-shaped tools that fitted little in the machinery of life. And what they had to unlearn was considerable; they had to loosen their tenseness of eager competition in an endeavor to fit within a society aiming at cooperation.

:-:

In a free society a school that favors the gifted to the detriment of the others is highly immoral.

What would you say to a school in which only the pretty girls and handsome boys would be the recipients of medals and scrolls, and the ugly ones put under a dunce cap or even publicly expelled?

What would you say to a school where only the slim girls and boys would receive the good marks, while the others would be marked low or kicked out? What would you say to a school in which only the redheads would be rewarded?

A pupil can as little help being quick on the trigger or having a lasting memory as he or she can help being good of looks, slim of frame or endowed with a shock of reddish hair. This, in my opinion, is the cardinal and cruel mistake perpetrated by an ancient system of education in which the allegedly gifted are rewarded and the less fortunate set back, despised and exposed to public ridicule. No man ever took the trouble of setting down the miseries which the young have to suffer through their school years because of the presence in their midst of those specially endowed by nature, whose endowment, as I mentioned before, most frequently is only of school duration. But that is a long time in the life of a growing child.

:-:

Does competition improve knowledge? I know it has often made for cribbing, for gross deceit; it has made for envy of schoolmates and antagonism toward teachers; it has made for anxiety, insecurity, and even malice against the lucky ones—but it has never improved true understanding.

You can pack a basketful of useless, and even some useful, information into a frightened head, but if you make it your business to follow up that child, you will find that most of it was tossed out posthaste, frequently right after the exam. And the little that remained could have readily been ensured by cooperative teaching instead of oppressive instruction.

:-:

What this world needs is not more of these hot-house plants that will wither anyhow at the first breath of fresh air from the open. What this world needs is deep thought about the problem of how to raise good people in a world beset by evil influence.

:-:

What is wrong with our schools in the south that a black man cannot find twelve among his white peers even to indict his son's slayers, that a black woman cannot find a judge even to listen to her tale of kidnaping and torture?

I have already told you what is wrong with all those schools: They have taken God out of the schools and left the devil in them—the devil of arrogance, the devil of prejudice, the devil of greed and the devil of denunciation and the devil of aggressiveness, the devil of subservience and the devil of egotism.

They have taken out of school the God of the book of Moses, the God that is love; the God of King David, the God that is generosity; and the God of King Solomon, the God that is humility. They teach you a hundred subjects in these schools—everything except ethics, the art of being human, the art of being humane.

Science

Excepting medicine, science has enhanced our lives with little comfort that wasn't thrice outweighed by bloody damage, be it by powder, plane or atom.

:-:

Some fight religion in the name of science; on closer inspection, both seem to have eluded them.

:-:

Man's ax got sharper, not his wit.

:-:

Knowledge makes man neither free nor good. The Romans, most learned of ancient peoples, tolerated Caligula and Nero, and enthusiastical- ly carried the scourge of the Fasces into peaceful neighboring lands. The Germans, most learned of the twentieth century, elected a paranoiac housepainter as chancellor and tumbled glee- fully from executions to death-camps and back.

Knowledge and science are tools that can be used for evil as readily as for good. The scientist or scholar is not made a better man by his knowledge, only a more dangerous one.

:-:

Perhaps science has harnessed enough of the powers of nature; let us now harness the powers of science.

:-:

Science began with a gadget and a trick. The gadget was the wheel; the trick was fire. We have come a long way from the two-wheel cart to the round-the-world transport plane, or from the sparking flint to man-made nuclear fission. Yet I wonder whether the inhabitants of Hiro- shima were more aware of the evolution of

science than ancient man facing an on-storming
battle chariot.

It isn't physics that will make this a better
life, nor chemistry, nor sociology. Physics may
be used to atom-bomb a nation and chemistry
may be used to poison a city and sociology has
been used to drive people and classes against
classes. Science is only an instrument, no more
than stick or fire or water that can be used to
lean on or light or refresh, and also can be used
to flail or burn or drown. Knowledge without
morals is a beast on the loose.

:-:

Science is hidden behind a tight web. Every
so often someone unravels a tiny thread, getting
a glimpse into her mysteries. A thousand riddles
are still far away from our peepholes.

:-:

They teach what science has accomplished.
They need to tell also, and more so, the unfinished business of science, the long index of
matters unknown and problems unsolved.

:-:

In their rush for new comforts and expediency scientists have left man's peace of mind

where it was when they started three thousand years ago.

:-:

Whatever science and its education has inspired, it has not strengthened the voice of humanity and not helped the weak in distress.

Science serves the wicked as readily as the well-meaning. Often we have witnessed the flight of scientists from lands of freedom like our own, England, or France to countries where vitriolic tyrants governed. Some did not flee to the dictator's lair; they prefer, rather, to remain in the security of our democracies while doing the enemy's bidding by whitewashing his crimson shield and besmirching the banner of their native country. Thus they live vicariously in the nimbus of the totalitarian overlord, sometimes encouraged by Stalin prizes and Hitler medals, at other times repaid in ways not yet known.

:-:

Science has taken the place of the Church. Once the Church built magnificent cathedrals in the midst of serf hovels and starving townships; science now is widely expanding in most luxurious space adventures while more than half of the world's population eke out a pauper's dread and diseased existence.

:-:

The wisdom of love, the knowledge that goodness to fellowman is the fundamental principle of human society, is as rarely introduced into our schools as it is into our politics or our churches, regardless of creed. Man can get along with much less science than he has today. As it is, very little of it goes into the healing crafts and so much of it into machinery of destruction.

We live no better together on this globe in our time than the cavemen did a hundred thousand years ago; and we have massacred in our generation many more people than in all previous known history.

Science certainly is not the answer to our great problems—not by a missile shot. Science may bind a few wounds, but then again, it will cut many more gashes.

:-:

We have had Nobel prize-winners behave like Casablanca barroom agents and scientists with illustrious names shame the muses all in one. Science can be less a step toward culture than an impediment to humaneness. The Nobel prize-winners were as ready to make an atom bomb for Hitler, and they almost succeeded, as they were to do later for Mao.

Scientist

Seems to be a title reserved not for the philosophers and those who study human nature, conduct, ethics, history and faith—but solely for those who work in rocket fuel, atomic fission and plastics.

Scripture

Some swear by God's scripture but act by the Devil's script.

God never wrote books, nor did His sons. From the way in which so many people in the Western World regard God, one must assume He was a Jew who spoke Hebrew only, although some Scriptures are written in Aramaic. But what of the rest of the world? Most people in India and China and South Asian countries do not even know there is a Hebrew language; still they revere Scriptures and other messages of God.

In my eyes it shows rather short-sighted thinking to attribute to the good Lord only such very recent religious documents as those available in the early antiquity of Eurasia. I have always resented the idea of degrading the good Lord to the rank of an editor of priestly documents.

Second Childhood
The old seem to be in second childhood because they have learned that much of life is better taken as a game than a gauntlet.

Security
Is a blessing, but not if bought at the expense of fellow man.

Self-Confidence
Does not always bring a man to the top, but no one ever got there without it.

Self-Esteem
Think of yourself as you wish others to think of you.

Self-Government
Perhaps some of the less modern nations do not yet know how to govern themselves, but their colonial masters have certainly proven they cannot do it for them.

Self-Improvement
There is no short cut to self-improvement away from the main road of world betterment.

Selfishness

All men are selfish, but how their selves differ!

:-:

Selfishness is a commendable instinct, if man would only find his true self.

Self-Knowledge

Everyone knows himself best, but refuses to admit it for fear of incrimination.

Self-Reliance

Better to be wise with the help of seven sages than aimlessly drifting on your own power.

:-:

It does not matter if you got there by pulling yourself up by your bootstraps or with the help of your fellow man as long as you are out of the mud.

:-:

Men who want no help are men who give no help.

Sense of Humor

To laugh at oneself is both wit and wisdom.

Serenity

Those who have not found a spiritual harbor in which to anchor their thoughts find themselves adrift at every squall.

:-:

Many who display in life and before your face a placid serenity may be harboring a volcano of turmoil. One may know a man all his life and never know him at all.

Sermon

The flocks should leave impressed by the Lord, not by the Rabbi.

:-:

Their sermons spill over with honey; still they have given to the world but the cup of bitterness.

Servility

Is a form of inverted arrogance.

:-:

Those who bow to the man above will invariably step on the man below.

:-:

One can show off poverty as well as riches,

neglect as well as cleanliness. Quite a few saintly persons appear to have considered dirtiness next to Godliness. To me, the beggar with rips in his cloak, the medieval itinerant preacher who kissed the sores of the stricken, who washed not, to rebuke vanity, was perhaps the most vain of them all. He brags with his neglect as brazenly as the bon vivant with his incense for the Lord and his sinecure.

The posture of the ascetics, the beggars, or any other of the overbearing flagellant and hirsute braggadocios is an expression not of profound religious feeling, but rather of an insufferably vain personage, incapable or unwilling to travel the broad road of accomplishment. They attempt to take a short cut to the heaven of recognition by prostration and self-humiliation.

The gate to religious wisdom lies in serenity and not in servility.

Sex

Was always here but never so much talked about.

:-:

If it were man's dominant motive, then the peasant who conducts his sex life on the level

332 |

of stable husbandry could be considered its best-adjusted master.

:-:

Sex, of course, is part of living, but some of our literati are making living part of sex.

:-:

The evil in the world is not done by those who fornicate, but by hateful and hate-spreading, vicious little men who as often as not have their sex under control, but not their gall.

Hitler lived in almost perfect abstinence and monstrous Philip II of Spain, who forbade victims of the Inquisition the little privilege of being garroted before being slowly burned alive ("so they may feel the full wrath of God"), never practiced sex except for procreation and died covered with holy amulets and missal in hand.

One can do an awful lot of evil and have a spotless sex life, and one can burn up the springs of desire and still do good to the rest of the world.

Shepherd
Church professionals like to play **God** when they should play shepherd.

Shrewdness

Experience makes for shrewdness; it's the heart that makes for wisdom.

Sickness

Some suffer more from their remedies than their illnesses.

Silence

May be golden, but sometimes it is only yellow.

:-:

Silence is the voice of the convinced; loudness is the voice of those who want to convince themselves.

:-:

It is not the stillness of the tongue that matters but the silence of the heart.

:-:

Silence is the gate to understanding.

Simplicity

The truly wise are always simple. It is the little mind that spins complications.

:-:

Simplicity is the garb of wisdom.

Sin

Is sweet. Were it not, it would not be necessary to prohibit it.

:-:

Sin is the weak man's failing, the strong man's secret.

:-:

A man's omissions are the measure of his deeds.

:-:

People blush at little sins, not at big crimes.

:-:

Blasphemy is not a sin, but a state of mind; self-abuse is not a sin, but lack of mental hygiene; fornication is not a sin, but a style of life; homosexuality is not a sin, but a sickness; heresy is not a sin, but a parting of the ways; vanity is not a sin, but lack of insight—I could go on and list a great number of paragraphs in the religious code of sin that need expunging, but then there would be very little left of this troublesome piece of ecclesiastic jurisprudence, and perhaps they would have to put away entirely their manuals of penance.

Sin occurs if you hurt your fellow man; nothing else is sinful, though it might be foolish or feeble.

Sinners

Lead an interesting life but wind up with loss of their capital.

Skepticism

Be quick to doubt and you hasten reason.

:-:

Skepticism is only an approach to sagacity, not wisdom itself.

Sky

Is just an ocean of gases in which trillions of minute creatures are floating; they swarm around the tasty globe like gnats around a cut fruit, these ubiquitous tiny beasts, infecting man, animal and plant.

Slave Traders

The most callous traders of the eighteenth century were the German rulers, who sold the sons of their peasants and poor into forced military service to England.

Slavery

It is shocking that the philosophers who dominated the Western mind for two thousand years, Plato and Aristotle, upheld slavery as a God-given institution.

Slavery was certainly not born with Plato and Aristotle. But their books justified, to an adulating Europe of so-called Christian faith, the idea that some were born free and some born slaves.

The fantastic situation lies in the utter indifference of the Christian world to the obvious contradictions existing between the teachings of Christ about the equality of men and the prevalent enslavement of serfs, bondsmen, and kidnaped blacks by Christians.

The freeing of slaves, tragically enough, was not done by, but in spite of, the Church.

:-:

The slave's chains are still there; yesterday, about his neck; today, about his mind.

:-:

How the church misread the mountain sermon of the gentle Jew who said, "Blessed are the poor in heart." Saint Paul exhorted slaves to be content with their station in life. The later Church fathers pacified resentment among

| 337

the slaves by pointing to it as a consequence of original sin. Bishop Ambrose argued that slaves were blessed with a better opportunity to practice the Christian virtue of humility. Another one, the saintly Isidore, pointedly remarked that at the Last Judgment the slave has an advantage over the free man by being able to pass off responsibility for his own sins to his masters.

The great Saint Augustine, author of *The City of God,* the book that for a thousand years held up the glory of Rome as above everything worldly, called upon slaves to serve obediently even wicked masters, because their slavery was the result of sin.

:-:

Christianity in general made a poor case, if any, against enslavement of pagans or Christians. Somehow it seems as if the Christian churches would rather lean heavily in favor of the ruler than the unruly.

:-:

The landed clergy of Spain and England, France and Germany, defended slavery, along with all the other arrogations of royalty, as a God-ordained institution. The multiple abuses of feudalism went on for a hundred generations without criticism from the Christian Church.

Some of the men of the black cloth even went into apologetics about *jus primae noctis,* the right of the feudal lord to take the bride of any of his serfs for himself on her wedding night. Bede relates in his famous *History* that the English nobles in his time would take any of the serf women for their pleasure whenever they were thus inclined, then sold them at a good price when they became pregnant.

:-:

Frederick the Great on his deathbed said, "I am tired of ruling over slaves." His slaves, however, had already said when he assumed the throne, "We are tired of being slaves to the King."

Sleep
Perhaps it is Sleep that, in replenishing the body energies, saps our strength. Is that why they call him the brother of Death?

Slogan
A slogan is often more effective than a treatise.

Smile
A smile is still the best make-up for a face.

:-:

The flag of truce in a world of strife.

:-:

The manner of wisdom.

:-:

Smile! If only for the lift it gives your company.

:-:

Smiles will turn no torrent nor smooth a tempest into zephyr, but they make the journey so much pleasanter.

Snobbery

Is an attitude of infantile forgetfulness—forgetfulness that in this fleeting ocean of life all these man-made distinctions born of petty desire, created by smallish minds, are mere pebbles over which the water-mountains float endlessly, majestically.

:-:

You can't pull rank on God. No man walks past Saint Peter's gate with a monocle in his face.

Social Theories

It may be argued that social theories work out well in book and pamphlet but not in the field or the factory. I am inclined to say that if the social theories of Karl Marx do not work out well in the practice of living, they were false to begin with in book and pamphlet.

Socialism

The blueprint of paradise over a foundation of purgatory.

:-:

The shamefaced cousin of Communism, losing virtue by kinship rather than misdeed.

Socialists

Were almost to a man anti-Semitic: Proudhon, Marx, Fourier, Engels, Lassalle, Bakunin, Stalin, Khrushchev. The Christian theologians have for so long preached the legend of the Jew as moneychanger that even the opponents of the churches learned to accept the Jew as a symbol of cunning capitalism.

The Socialists (including the German National Socialists) found in this sickly symbolism an attractive appeal to the populace of Western Europe, for thousands of years nurtured in their churches on the incessant ritualization of the Jew as accursed Christ killer and profiteer in thirty pieces of silver.

| 341

Society

The clue to a man's true nature is the character of his enemies.

Socrates

Socrates was put to the hemlock not because of professing a new truth; rather because he pilloried the old conventional lies.

Solipsism

Perhaps the whole wide world is only in our mind. In that case, let's have an orderly mind!

Solitude

Is a state of mind, not a geographic position. There are no lonelier places than certain spots in certain crowds.

:-:

Solitude: alone with a throng of phantoms and the kaleidoscope of imagination.

Sophisticate

A person who derides all standards in order to avoid the job of studying them.

:-:

Wisdom by necessity will "no" some things and "yes" others; the frivolous steal the nimbus of wisdom by deriding all and sundry.

Sophistication

Cracking a thought into a joke.

Sorrow

Is the messenger of friendship.

Soul

Souls must lead a harrowed life within the stormy body-complex of cells and blood and nerves.

:-:

It takes all the skill of steady husbandry to raise a soul to bloom; most of them lead a stunted existence and wilt before their petals open up.

Soul-Doctors

Help should be given to those who deserve it, not those who can afford it.

:-:

So many search the souls of others who have yet to look into their own.

Space Travel

We are morally in no better position attempting to visit other planets than the murderous goldhunters Cortez and Pizarro. We are a nefarious lot with a record of forty million killings in the last few decades alone. What have we to offer? A globe that has not learned in a million years to govern itself and still feels ready to strike out for new territory.

:-:

It seems the Marsmen have a stronger appeal to the civic purseholders than the poverty-stricken and diseased masses: it is easier to get a billion for space than a million for earth.

Speech
Don't judge a man until you have heard him speak. The voice is the truest mirror of mind and intent.

Spinoza
Thought so little of the public mind that he eschewed reputation.

Spirit
Is the spice of life. It is *Shechinah,* the Hebrew for the living God. Of course one can live a whole existence on a spiceless diet.

Staff of Life
A man's soul feeds on either love or hate.

Some live on the pleasures of the good deed; others are of such disposition that only doing hurt and harm will nourish them. Ormuzd and Ahriman.

So many live on a diet of hate, cherishing envy and greed like satiating herbs, while love is shunned like a poison. These cannibals of the soul have infested the caves, tents and roofs of all the continents. They have made man cry out in anguish of war and torment since the birth of Adam.

But somehow there always rose those who would bear the symbols of the Lord and stretch out their arms in beatitude.

Stars

Some appear to their contemporaries as already having the touch of eternity, but eternity may choose a little man from the side lines. The great luminaries come and go, while some little star becomes fixed.

Statesman

The path of the statesman is haunted by politicians—starlings in the flight of the eagle.

:-:

Statesmen see themselves as handmaidens of

history; politicians see the state as a handmaiden of themselves.

Statues
There are too many on horseback. I would like to see more standing on the sod, at the lathe or beside a desk.

Stone of Wisdom
Find charity and you have found the stone of wisdom. Truth is the sagacity of the heart, and out of hate can grow no understanding.

Stupidity
Is sometimes more of a defense than a characteristic.

Style
Some persons forgot to put on this season's opinions and now everybody thinks they are old-fashioned.

:-:

Mind makes the style, not vice versa.

:-:

Some writers overwhelm the reader with the beauty of their style. One has to read them a second time to be sober enough to judge what they really mean.

Subsistence
The common beast spends far less time in obtaining its means of subsistence than erudite man.

Success
I know of no greater failure than the man who devotes his life to the achievement of success.

:-:

The man who sets success as his goal is doomed to failure, since one desire for achievement succeeds another in the endless chain of human vanity.

:-:

Fancy props don't make up for a shoddy play.

Suffering
Will hearten some and harden others.

Suicide
To die at one's own hand may be of more grace than living in subjugation or disease.

:-:

There is a commandment "Thou shalt not kill," but none "Thou shalt not die."

:-:

A man has the right to commit homicide in self-defense, and a man has the right to commit suicide in defense of a cause or issue greater than himself.

The Sun
It is not earth that is mother of man, but the sun. The sun gives its nourishing rays to the plants, which man and his animal food live on; the sun evaporates the water that filters into man's springs; the sun warms the air man breathes and the ground he walks on. Man is truly a child of the sun. Still, whence does Helios draw its matter and energy? Wherefrom the unknown and perhaps peregrine donor?

:-:

The energies that carry this our globe and billions like it through space and time are breath-taking. And this is but the tiny universe that our tiny cornea envisions.

What mysterious other attributes must that Unknown Eternal possess that we call with the ancient nomen: God. Perhaps the Hebrews were right in warning: Name it naught but the Eternal, the One.

The Sun is what you make it—the Light of Lights or just an extension of bursting gases.

Sunday Schools
Are the places where Christian children learn to hate before they learn to read. Already the littlest ones have been told that the Jews are the killers of God, and thus they know the Jews as criminals before they meet the Jews as people.

Superiority
There are no people with a superiority feeling, only those with an uncontrolled desire to hide their inferiority.

Superstition
Is the anteroom to religion where those remain who cannot get an audience with their own selves.

Suspicion
May as well be the gate to knowledge as to hate.

Suttee
The now obsolete Hindu practice of burning

widows exemplifies the petrification of moral principles. In earlier scriptures of Hinduism there is a solemn plea for connubial devotion beyond the grave.

Swearing
   Is better than sulking.

Symbols
   Words are only symbols; if those who argue only realized how little they differed in facts!

Sympathy
   Arguments may win the day but sympathy will win the man.

T

Tale

Truth is so hard to tell, it sometimes needs fiction to make it plausible.

Talk

Deep-bottomed boats travel slowly.

:-:

Talk is primarily a way of killing time. Perhaps that explains its popularity.

:-:

Mankind divides itself into two types: dialogue people and monologue people: The latter never hear you or your side since they are pauseless monologists.

:-:

A peasant may be more interesting than a scholar if the peasant opens his soul and the scholar only an odd book.

:-:

Though you don't hear the fish, it doesn't mean they are not talking.

:-:

Some talk of a thousand different things and still speak only about themselves.

:-:

Men differ much more in talk than in thought.

Taste
Is the feeler of man's appetite and still the best judge of right nutrition.

:-:

Taste is spoiled in childhood by parental prejudice and in adults by customs and fads.

Teachers
The job of the teacher is to bring out what's in the pupil, not pour in what's in his manual.

:-:

No teacher has the right to stigmatize a child as being inferior because its memory is weaker than that of others. No teacher has the right to mark a child low or lower because its apparatus of comprehension works slower than that of others. No teacher has the right to point out the child or mark it publicly because its strength of comprehension or span of attention operates on a different depth or length.

If anyone objects to my using the term "publicly," may I explain that to the pupil his colleagues and friends in the classroom are his peers, that is, his public, as your colleagues and friends are your public. He has to spend ten or twenty years of his life in the classroom, labeled by public tests and public evaluations an inferior individual.

How would you like being, let's say a physician if your bag and your car were marked "Rather Mediocre Doctor"? Or a lawyer if your briefcase were stamped "Barely 60—Sloppy—A Shyster"? Or then again, considering also those on the other side of the fence, how would you like being a pharmacist if you had to post over your shop a sign reading in loud, red letters "Terrific Chap—A Genius"? Or a housewife who had to walk about the house in an apron inscribed "Wonderful Cook—Magnificent Breeder"?

Under conditions similar to these, unbelievable as it seems, do our youngsters have to spend the first twenty-odd years of their lives.

:-:

We have had teachers for the Crown's sake, teachers for God's sake, teachers for Science's sake, teachers for Business' sake, but none yet for man's sake.

Tears
Come readily from shallow souls.

:-:

Blessed the tears shed for the brother's woe and the smile over the neighbor's happiness!

Teleology
If man is nature's ultimate goal then this is an awfully small world.

:-:

Man is as little the final purpose of divine providence as an elk or a beetle or a salamander.

:-:

Teleology in its attempts to find a man-suiting purpose in nature will have to contend with the teleology of plants, animals and perhaps other entities.

Were the sunflowers placed in the meadow as supply source for the bees; or as food for some parasites; or for man to look at; or to drop to the ground and serve as fertilizer for surrounding weeds?

What a tragicomic pose! Tiny man no bigger than a mold traveling on a gigantic rock through billions of years and miles in an unfathomed galaxy of innumerable worlds, yet hollering at the top of his inaudible voice: Hear me, trillions of universes, aeons of times, infinites of space! I, man, earthbound fungus, 98 per cent water, 2 per cent phosphorus and such, I am the aim and end of it all. I am the purpose of all this majestic movement in its mysterious history!

Perhaps the Torah was right in forbidding man to set himself in stone or paint, lest he feel himself lasting or even everlasting. Is he more than a pinch of dust with a whisper of breath?

:-:

If there be purpose to this world in its crazy meandering, it can't be a good one. By all human reckoning there is more sin harvested in a day than goodness planted in a year.

Temper

Let your thoughts be burning, but your words cool.

:-:

Watch your voice and you need not watch your words.

Theodicy

Not all is good and beautiful in this world, but then neither are we.

:-:

We find a spider web glistening in the morning dew enchantingly aesthetic—yet it is only the shroud of a still-kicking victim. The nightingale breaks into a delightful cadence of song whenever her golden throat swallows the crushed worm; and who has not admired the picture of leonine majesty resting satiated in the bush, a limp half-eaten doe under his mighty paw. The world seems ordained to mutual destruction in a chain of necessities.

:-:

What sad predestination: heroes and sages put to death by the bite of an invisible bug. And the bug lives on.

Theology of Hate

A religious doctrine must be not only true but also helpful. The Christian theology is the only one among many that has built in its very canon a testament of hate against a whole people, the Jewish nation. The Christian theology represents itself to the wide world through the symbol of the Roman gallows of the crucifix, condemning systematically the Hebrews as killers of God.

It seems as if the Christian religion of love cannot uphold itself at all without the canonical thesis of hate and condemnation.

Thinking

Thought is a twig on the tree of emotion and instinct. As it was a million years ago, the first is still an outgrowth of the latter.

:-:

Men think quite alike; if it were different, they could not coexist even for a day. But most people judge by traditional or imitated judgment patterns, and snap judgments are the rule and the rulers.

:-:

How come the sages of all times speak the same truth? The Hebrews revere *Shalshelet Ha Cabbalah*, the Chain of Tradition. There is a chain of tradition running from the days of Ur to our time, but familiarity with the so-oft-repeated pronouncements of the prophets has estranged us. Perhaps the sayings of our fathers should be translated into a foreign idiom and then brought back as a rare find, in order to be listened to again!

:-:

Is thinking ever free? Wherever I meet it, I find it chained to a *motive* of one kind or another. The world operates on motivated thinking tied to prejudice, opportunism, greed, narrow-mindedness, selfishness, and a thousand other little passions and passionettes that clutter up the narrow path of righteousness.

:-:

Thinking can be shaped by heart, gall, glands, stomach, or even shifting eyes. Sometimes I wish that people's thoughts came in colors so one could see what part of the body sent them forth.

:-:

Thinking may be classified on a color chart, however, of poetic imagination. Some people's cogitations run rosy; others gray, even black. There are those who think yellow and those who live and breathe blood red. The minds of others are of peculiar color combinations. And there are sages whose badge is white, embodying all the colors. No human emotion is strange to them, yet none colors their thoughts.

:-:

A good thought, even when poorly presented, will finally emerge right side up.

:-:

The last thought is always wiser than the first.

:-:

The two most important subjects in the world are totally neglected in our schools, namely, thinking and ethics. They teach the Latin names of the bones of a reptile or the names of unavailable plants. They teach fanciful mathematical abstractions, of the uselessness of which the practical men in the field bitterly complain. They teach hypothetical hundred-million-year data in paleontology and geology, which every five years are thrown aside. They teach multiple statistics of city and town, populations of faraway nations and continents. They give verbose interpretations of the hidden meanings of a spotted canvas presented by cunning abstractionists. They teach you the crown and land robberies perpetrated by all the kings, despots and dictators of their hemisphere; they make you learn by rote the individual battles these usurpers lost or won, the mistresses they kept, the aristocratic kinfolk they obliterated, etc., etc. But they don't teach you how to think and think out clearly an alleged fact presented before you, how to recognize prejudice from judgment, how to recognize traditional nonsense from reality, and how to bring ethics into life and how to be kind and understanding, tolerant and generous to your fellow creature.

Perhaps they tell you that ethics and thinking should be taught by parents and the church, but you and I know, judging by past history, that the churches have a habit of traveling with the rulers, and so far as thinking of the parents is concerned, it is exactly that which more often you have to overcome than abide by.

:-:

They are not thinking, they are being thought for.

In order to think, man must first extricate himself from the web of traditional thought patterns. He must learn to swim, not just float.

:-:

If the thinking of the world is to be improved by education then the schools must regard it as a prime obligation to change the emotional outlook of the pupils in order to correct their thinking. If the children in Peking, Moscow and Havana are instilled with hate against the people of America their later thinking will breathe that hate. And the nefarious ideologies of their hidden masters will seem to the youth as logical as the ethics of cooperation appear to those who live and study in true democracy and true freedom.

:-:

To make children think straight one must make them feel right.

A child filled with hate, envy and arrogance will by necessity become imbued with the logic of intolerance and prejudice.

Snobbism has its logic just as civility has. The logic is the same. It is the mental activation of the body and can reason for its emotional master —greed and arrogance—in the same way that the logic of the benevolent will reason on behalf of goodness and toleration. The world has acquired a tremendous amount of knowledge in the last 500 years but has not become better for it because this knowledge, concentrated in science and technology, improved little but speed and comfort. Man's conduct toward man has hardly improved. Indeed one is almost inclined to assume that science and technology are primarily in the service of destruction. No matter what share of the national income the major countries of the world may have allotted to science, we are safe in assuming that it is mainly devoted to war science, while only the crumbs fall to medicine and other fields of scientific welfare. Science without humanistic direction is not beneficial but rather dangerous.

:-:

It is impossible to improve a person's thinking, as impossible as it is to improve a man's heartbeat or the functions of his intestines. However, as in the case of the physical functions, one can avoid the consumption of indigestible or bad food.

Like the body, of course, the mind differs from person to person in intensity, in capacity, in range, depth and tendency to disintegration. But fundamentally, all minds work alike, just as all livers work alike, all kidneys work alike, all hearts work alike, all stomachs work alike.

To retain a healthy mind, one need do no more than avoid the absorption of negativistic motivation.

:-:

For thousands of years the minds of men have been defiled by evil motivation introduced from the outside; men have learned to judge issues, people and events, not by reason, but by the opportune patterns set by their oppressors.

:-:

Don't teach the student how to write correctly. Teach him how to think correctly. The writing will follow, and if not, so much the better. We can well do with less writing and more thinking.

:-:

A thought is given for a specific purpose, like a drug; it often, however, goes its own unforeseen way.

Time

Time does not heal wounds, it just hides some and deepens others.

:-:

How quickly does today turn into yesterday.

:-:

Time took the wrong road. The Past was not all glory; there was wilderness. But now we are trapped in a Death Valley with no sight of a Tomorrow.

:-:

No one can plot the path of time; perhaps

we have been standing on a byway for centuries,
thinking our dead end was the summit of it all.

Time and Space

Live on borrowed existence: they are not
really there, they just relate to each other.

Today

Is to be lived as if it were tomorrow, because
tomorrow is only belated yesterday.

Tolerance

Must stop at the threshold of monstrosity.

:-:

Tolerance appears in two editions, one bound
in wisdom and one in indifference.

:-:

Tolerance is ill used on friends of the great
sinners. When the sinners fall, some of their
friends plead the thin excuse of compulsion.
The sycophants are always ready to serve the
new master and renounce the old, but the Hebrews said you cannot be Abaddon, angel of the
bottomless pit, and Gabriel in one person.

:-:

Study history as to the minor infractions for

which offenders were burned a few hundred
years ago, and thank your fate for living today
and not then.

Not that the churches have lost their attitude;
they have only lost their power.

Tombstone

Better study your epitaph now lest your
tombstone belie its dead.

Tomorrow

If a tomorrow were never to come, it would
not be worth living today.

:-:

Don't hope for a better tomorrow unless you
help it to become so.

:-:

So much time is given to the study of yesteryear, so little, pitifully little, to the study of
tomorrow.

Tongue

The tongue is man's best friend but also his
worst enemy.

:-:

The pen may be mightier than the sword but

mightier yet is the tongue. The tongue-waggers are the masters of our era, the Hitlers, the Maos, the Mussolinis. The swish of their tongues is deadlier than all weapons.

:-:

Buddhists attribute four evils to the tongue—slander, lying, idle talk and offensive speech—and only three to the rest of the body. By their words you shall judge them. Vicious tongues have incited to world-wide massacre and have ever so much prejudiced thinking among men and nations, races and creeds.

Torture

Nature is beset with suffering, but of all beasts, only man makes a business of prolonging it.

Totalitarianism

This granite earth we live on could be a bed of roses were it not for the scheming Procrustes and his fellow henchmen, be their shirts black, brown or red.

:-:

The Red camarilla has taken the romance out of socialism and replaced it with opportunistic expediency, thus losing the best of the idea and acquiring the worst that is in imperialist government.

Tradition

Tradition implies carryover from the past. And who is so little acquainted with history and unaware how horrible the past was and how young the centuries are in which at least part of mankind has been living in freedom?

Up to the decades of the American and French Revolutions most of the inhabitants of the Western and Eastern world lived in an abysmal state of servitude. The villeins of England, the hoerige of Prussia, the serfs of Russia, the old peasantry and much of labor, and even the so-called white-collar classes lived in complete dependence upon the despotic rulers who treated them as part of their immense holdings—no better than private property. A tasteless remnant of this era is reference to the citizens of England as the "subjects" of the king.

:-:

The lord of the manor was the sole employer, the judge and the domineering authority over body and soul of the common man in Europe up to the eighteenth century. In many parts of Asia this system still prevails.

| 367

In our own country a bare hundred years ago our grandfathers and great-grandfathers were selling people in the open market place on the same platform with pigs and goats and cucumbers.

Nay, "tradition" is an implicated word and should be rarely put to use, and then most cautiously.

And the churches we belong to. It is only a few hundred years since our churches burned Quakers in London, hanged witches in New England and garroted heretics in Portugal, Brazil and Mexico. It is better to look forward than backward. Our past is black and bloody. Let the future be clear and clean.

Training

You cannot train a horse with shouts and expect it to obey a whisper.

Travel

People travel to faraway places to watch, in fascination, the kind of people they ignore at home.

Treason

Once a traitor, always a question mark.

The Tree

Is the symbol of wisdom: it never shouts, and only whispers when it's moved.

Trite

We call the oft-repeated truism which we have accepted for the record but never for real —for example, Love thy neighbor.

Trust

Is an expectation based more on the hopes of the person having it than on the nature of the one trusted. No one is so deceitful that he has not been trusted by some and sundry.

Truth

Appears in many faces, seldom in its own.

:-:

To judge truth by its expediency is like calculating the profits of love.

:-:

All men can savor truth, but it has to be served differently from one to another.

:-:

Man's mind is confounded by the deceitful twins: hearsay and gainsay.

:-:

Truth drops its wings before a low-ceilinged mind.

:-:

Truth hurts only the liar.

:-:

Truth may not make you free but falsehood will enslave you.

:-:

People spend more time on camouflaging truth than in uncovering it.

Tyranny
Is tyranny, no matter what banner is flown from the halberd.

U

Ugliness

Little ugliness fills the air of our society like insects. They don't kill you, but they make life miserable.

:-:

Ugly faces suffer little temptation.

Unconscious

Man is pretty well aware of which currents course through his gray matter; he conceals them so well, however, that it is his neighbor who remains unconscious of their existence.

:-:

Man is an open book, but he does not care to have you read over his shoulder.

Understanding

Exists on infinite levels. A moth comprehends the candle light, so do a dog and a bird; an infant figures it out, so do savage and savant. There are infinite attributes to all manifestations of the universe and endless variations of conception.

:-:

It matters little whether people misunderstand you, as long as you don't misunderstand them.

Unity

Being united is not necessarily a virtuous act; the devils, too, work in unison.

Universe

To find order in the cosmos is fundamental, but beyond our concept of the universe looms a greater one.

:-:

Man resides on his little globe like a coral in a tiny, lost pool; the great waves of the mother ocean hardly ever reach his shores.

:-:

We know there are rhythms in the cosmos but who keeps the beat and what is the score?

:-:

There is more mystery in the yolk of an egg

than in a galaxy of planets, if we could only fathom it.

:-:

Universe is only the little cosmos we see with eye and telescope. Beyond the beyond is *Pantaverse*, the endless worlds of worlds—*Ain Soph*, the Cabbalists named it, the One Without End.

Unpleasantness
With some, it is just a way of giving themselves airs.

Untouchables
There are at least three or four hundred castes in India. Less than one-fifth of the population belongs to the three high castes, but so great is the power of spoken and written words that no matter how contrary these words are to reality, the priests manage to persuade the people, their teachers, their governments and even their educated segments that the caste system is a divine ordination of life-after-death-in-life. The untouchables themselves have been persuaded that they must pay by painful reincarnation for their prenatal offenses. What fools these mortals be.

Utopia
No promise or hope of tomorrow's better world is worth the price of today's liberty.

Valor

Is a matter of the mind. It is in the choice of purpose that valor differs from recklessness.

:-:

Valor is measured by the height of the cause not the heat of the battle.

Vanitas

If only the conquerers realized in time that their deeds are a game with worthless chips. After taking all the mountains and seas, they wind up like everybody else with a muddy slab of stone and their name on it.

Vanity

Can work through a display of poverty as well as through a show of wealth.

:-:

Vanity has no greater offender than the one who flaunts his indifference.

:-:

Vanity is no sin, resignation no virtue; ascetics have lit fagots under fellow creatures and dandies have fallen in defense of the innocent.

:-:

The Beau Brummell and the ragged hermit who ostentatiously squats in front of his cave are two of the same kind. In both, vanity is the master. Vanity can glow from the silver knob of a fancy cane, and vanity can shine through the rips of a soiled "holy man's" cloak.

Vatican Betrayal

For a hundred days and three years they published plans and schemes to free the Jew from the burden of defamation as alleged killers of Christ.

When the time arrived to pen the resolve, they came out with the old adage: the Jews killed Christ.

Vegetarians

Like the whale, they prefer flesh of the invisible animals to that of the visible ones.

Venom

More people draw blood with a pen than with a knife.

Vice

Is a sickness rather than a sin; not the dissipating but the malevolent are damned.

Viewpoint

Some critics have berated me for judging from the Jewish point of view. Can the fish look upon the world from the aloofness of the seagull?

Virtue

Carries its own reward. Were this not so, only the superstitious would pretend to seek it, anticipating post mortem advantages. But true virtue, as well as true knowledge, is flavored by that rare beatitude called by the Hebrews *Simcha Shel Mitzwah*, "the pleasure of right."

:-:

Beware the one whose virtue lies in the fear of God and not in the love of man.

:-:

All sins are common to all people, but virtue is of the few.

:-:

Virtue lies not in kindness, but in constant kindness; even beasts commit single acts of generosity.

:-:

Virtue is the strength to do good in the face of evil.

:-:

The ancient Romans thought only man, *vir*, could be virtuous, implying that morality required strength, virility. How many men show strength in the face of injustice and then again how many so-called virtuous persons watch complacently while cruelty abounds? Mastering one's own alleged sins or sensualities takes small courage; virtue lies in opposing evil in the face of any circumstances. If the message of the Lord is helpfulness, then the calling of the Devil is indifference. We are all here either vicars of the Lord or vicars of Lucifer.

It is amazing that the creator of the domination of Catholicism, King Constantine, remained a pagan all his living days, and that Voltaire, the archenemy of Catholicism, never ceased being a Christian.

:-:

Virtue lies not in what one does to himself

or herself. Virtue lies in the long road where you act and react to your fellow men.

Vision

Some are so nearsighted they only see themselves.

Visionaries

Are often confused with pretenders who seem to run far ahead of progress itself, but in reality follow the clever course of compromise and conformism.

Voices

Rise and cease, yet the voice of silence speaks forever.

W

War

Is evil unless what it opposes is a still greater evil.

:-:

Living in appeasement under a dictator's yoke has all the sanguinary possibilities of war without the chance of redemption by battle.

:-:

War is not in the nature of man; defense is.

:-:

As far as the people themselves are concerned, they have little or nothing to gain by war, but everything—including their lives—to lose. In this sense, war is not in the nature of man, only in the nature of tyranny.

:-:

Wars of independence are but the inverted will for peace.

:-:

Perhaps the coming wars will be fought with pens instead of swords. The sting of the pen may be no less sharp than that of the edged weapon.

:-:

Little men who want to be remembered start great wars; great men who wish to be forgotten are the architects of peace.

:-:

Wars have changed their weapons but not their retribution.

:-:

Never in history have economic measures justified a war, although such cause has often been pretended; every war in history has been economically disastrous for all serious participants in it. Never in history have religious reasons justified a war, although religious pretense has occurred again and again.

Avaricious military adventurers, crusading buccaneers, gold-greedy pirates of land and sea, have often carried the long sword hidden under a religious banner. But no sooner did they spot the intended victim, than they dropped the standards of the ill-used Lord and stormed about their business of kill and plunder.

Genghis Khan and his wide banner on nine legs fell upon his neighboring lands under the guise of liberal nobility, just as Cortez, Pizarro and the others fell upon the Indians as latter-day apostles of the poor, ascetic Hebrew preacher Jesus.

:-:

Never was a neighbor puny enough not to have frightened the giant at the border into aggression.

History is filled with just wars of aggression, but never has aggression truly been just; similarly no robbery can be a deed of self-defense.

It is time to show the true face of history—the history of the people and not that of their exploiters, the history of free people who were made into slaves, the history of peaceable people who were vanished—and to show in their true light the persons of reckless ambition and malevolence who made the world we live in a jungle of mutual destruction for the glory and vanity and ugly avarice of the very few, their henchmen and their sycophants. From days so far back that for a record of them we have to dig for documents deep in the sands and at the bottom of the seas, to the very hour we live in, the evidence of evil can be heard and seen and it is no less horrible to behold today than it was in the past. Indeed, no outrage committed by the tyrants of old can outdo those perpetrated before our very eyes in this very generation. More people have been put to death—men, women and children—in the most grotesque manner by Hitler, Stalin and Mao during the lifetime of the reader of this book than have been slaughtered in all written history. Perhaps, if we clearly and solemnly look at the past, our vision of the present will be more concise.

:-:

The road to peace travels over the burial mound of dictatorship, and as long as we have dictatorship talk of peace will be no more than that. History has taught us that the more a dictator talks of peace, the closer he is to war.

Weakness
Is often goodness ill-received.

Wealth
Is no crime and poverty no virtue. Many who champion the cause of the poor live more like those they attack than those they defend.

:-:

Wealth of nations should be measured not only by the economy of material goods, but also by the resources in mind and heart. How poverty-stricken some of them are in their richness!

:-:

Wealth does not preclude virtue and poverty does not imply it.

:-:

It is folly to deride the planning for money in a world of insecurity. In a society of total security, the wish for wealth will recede of its own.

Well-Being
The well-being of a nation is not to be measured by its tranquility—a cemetery is quiet, too—but rather by the extent to which the masses of the people partake of the national wealth.

White Paper
Even the blackest nation finds it necessary to publish a White Paper.

Wickedness
Harbors often within those you least suspect.

Widowed

Some men become widowed while their wives are still alive, making a tomb of their homes.

Will

Riding the unbridled steed of passion thinks itself the master of the reins.

:-:

Will is awareness of a desire with a set of motivations more presupposed than comprehended.

Will Power

A tiny fraction only of man's actions are known to him. The thrust of the pulse, the rushing of the blood in a thousand veins and arteries, the flow of a hundred springs in glands and tissues, the chemical reactions in the transforming mechanisms of stomach, kidney, spleen and gall, the lighting of impulses in brain and nerve cells—a billion molecules within the framework of Homo sapiens are acting out a miniature universe, infested always by enemy microbes demolishing the very foundations of this thing called man.

Man's will controls only a minute fraction of the powers that move him.

Wisdom
Is a hermit. To find it you have to get off the beaten path.

:-:

There is a lot of foolishness in the wise and a lot of wisdom in the foolish.
Like victory, wisdom lies in the final outcome, not in the individual contest.

Wishing
Is the hurdle on the track of thinking.

Wit
May appear without wisdom; wisdom is never without wit.

Woman
Is not an equal but rather a sequel to man.

Women
So often confuse poseurs with pioneers. The retinue of most charlatans is nine women to one man, and about this one I am not always sure.

:-:

Women are the bearers of culture but not its makers. They read philosophy but do not write

it, play music but do not compose it, view art
and architecture but do not create it.

Words
Spoken by sect-ridden prophets and class-
strugglers have done more to divide people than
issues or things themselves.

:-:

Words offer a mine of information for those
who dig deep enough.

:-:

Words sometimes bring a rise to emotions;
at other times they just flatter them.

Work
The lowliest job can be made interesting and
the most exalted become a bore.

:-:

Work is man's most natural form of relaxa-
tion.

World
A chimaeric scheme of interconnecting gears
made up of living creatures who can exist only
by devouring each other.

:-:

The man who thinks this the best possible world has either little experience or little imagination.

:-:

The world will go on without you; give her something to remember you by, or at least wave at her kindly and with a good wish.

The World From Without

Think yourself gone, and the world, this world, without you; and then look at it quite detached. And that's how it will be soon enough.

How does the world strike you without yourself? Take this sober view and ponder.

World Government

Is wonderful; but first, where is that world?

Worship

Is either Judaic or Pagan, philosophical or idolatrous. The Hebrews worship no man, no saint, no priest, no face—only the *Echod*, the One, *Ain Soph*, the Infinite, *Elohim*, the Eternal.

The pagan, whatever his denomination, wants a man-god, a visible, walking, talking and personal god or goddess. He believes not in the invisible, he yearns for ikon and amulet, flesh and blood. But stone and flesh and blood and gold cannot fit the heart of man to the *Or Adonai,* the light of the Lord, in which we see Him with our love and conscience, in deeds of justice and charity; which deeds are the Alpha and Omega of true faith.

:-:

Be familiar with the Lord. Invite Him as often to your house as you visit His.

Writers
Are moved too much by the expectations of their public, rather than by their own momentum.

:-:

Some writers do an immense amount of traveling; they wander from darkness to darkness with impressive dispatch.

Writing
Whoever writes with ease carries little weight.

:-:

So many with nothing to say keep on saying it.

:-:

Wrongs

Were we to remember all wrongs done to us, we would live forever in hate.

:-:

A wrong forgotten is a wrong set right.

Y

Yes!
Is the first word from the lips of the Lord,
No! the first from the mouth of the Devil.

Youth
Is not indicative of progress, nor age of reaction.

:-:

Youth is only the beginning of old age.

:-:

Youth comes many times if the mind is kept aflow.

:-:

Nothing is more conducive to a youthful old age than a serene youth.

:-:

Youth may spot the failings of the old but often misses their virtues.

:-:

What impressed us long ago may have left our minds, but the impression has not.

:-:

It is better to die young than to live old.

:-:

Every age has its own beatitudes; those of youth can never be repeated although they are never forgotten.

Z

Zeal

The Lord is not in want of zealots, but of souls.

Zen

There are many shades of darkness, but only one principle of light. The experience of *Satori,* the enlightenment of Zen; the meditation into *Samahadi* of the Hindus; the *Tao* of Lao-tse, the road to inner self—they all are only different symbols signifying the Hebraic *Or Adonai,* the light of God which Spinoza so beautifully named *Amor Dei Intellectualis.*

Zero

They say that if all living humanity were placed body to body, they would fit into a cube no more than one mile in each dimension. One short mile out of the tens of thousands that make up this globe that, in turn, is just one battered rock out of billions of the kind we can see by eye and instrument.

Were one to visualize this one cubic mile of Homo sapiens sunk into a canyon or crater, what becomes of the world and worlds? The blades of grass would rise green as ever, the waves of the seven seas would storm and heave, the lava never cease its flow in the volcano and the starry skies not even blink at the anthill of humans, all gone out at once instead of in bunches.

That cubic mile of man is destined for burial in some canyon or crater, all two and a half billion segments of it, within a few fleeting decades, but, dropping to the ground, they leave their offspring for a like existence of passing fortune, which gives them the feeling of perennial life.

If all people were to be buried on one day and in one casket, instead of in billions of small interments, perhaps that thought would make them realize how much like planetary dust their life, how ludicrous their arrogant distinctions of race, class and what they call religion, which means "binding," but with most of them serves rather to separate than to unite.

Perhaps the day will come when this planetary dust that grew into flesh only to find its way back into a dugout of dust again, when this man of clay will truly reach awareness of his pitiful frailty and prove by deeds of charity and loving wisdom that somewhere, somehow in this mysterious universe there is a flame of godliness burning in aeonic distances and that a spark of this fire shimmers in the soul of man.

There is so little that we know even of what we can see about, beneath and above us, and what we can see is but a speck of the *Ain Soph*, the Endless, of which we can only dream in faint concepts.

Man's inhumanity to man has left its sanguinary mark upon the earth and waters of this globe since the days of earliest recollection. Forever some cunning creature would rise in piracy upon his neighbors and sway his tribe to carry out a nefarious scheme of pillage, rape and conquest.

If only those strutting evil little masters of some anthill of land would understand that with all their bluster, medals and fanfare, they too, are only clay on clay, and the dust of their graves is no respecter of tinsel and rank; and if the many who follow their power-usurpers on the bloody path of tyranny, if they, too, would learn it is better to lead a simple life on your feet than a fancy one on your knees.

If they would only understand that the pleas-

ures of humiliating others and holding neighbors in chains are as fleeting as the dust in the
wind—and that is all man is, dust in the wind
of time.

If they would only understand that there is
a serenity of the soul which comes with the
practice of kindness to man, a serenity which
outlasts the winds of time, since it is born in
the heart of hearts, where dwells the insight
into the majestic unity of this our universe.

You may call this God, or the voice of God;
we Hebrews call it *Echod, Adonai, Elohim,* the
One, the Lord, the Eternal.

Give it the name you will, this nameless One.
But let your deeds be in His grace and His
charity.